GOING . . . !
A Sacrifice?

Gal. 6:9

VERMEULEN

GOING . . . !
A Sacrifice?

A series of events and experiences
in the lives of the Vermeulen family
in the country of Suriname
South America.

A challenge to young and old to get involved
in serving Jesus Christ
across the world
in missionary endeavor.

Fred and Trudy

Copyright © 2017 by Fred and Trudy.

Library of Congress Control Number:		2017907190
ISBN:	Hardcover	978-1-5434-2155-2
	Softcover	978-1-5434-2154-5
	eBook	978-1-5434-2153-8

All rights reserved. No part of this book may be reproduced or transmitted in any form or by any means, electronic or mechanical, including photocopying, recording, or by any information storage and retrieval system, without permission in writing from the copyright owner.

Scripture quotations marked KJV are from the Holy Bible, King James Version (Authorized Version). First published in 1611. Quoted from the KJV Classic Reference Bible, Copyright © 1983 by The Zondervan Corporation.

Any people depicted in stock imagery provided by Thinkstock are models, and such images are being used for illustrative purposes only.
Certain stock imagery © Thinkstock.

Print information available on the last page.

Rev. date: 05/08/2017

To order additional copies of this book, contact:
Xlibris
1-888-795-4274
www.Xlibris.com
Orders@Xlibris.com
761951

Contents

Forewords vii
Acknowledgements xi

Chapter 1	Ministering in Different Places 1
Chapter 2	God's Leading to Suriname, 1960 4
Chapter 3	In Paramaribo 11
Chapter 4	Visits to Ricanau Moffo 15
Chapter 5	Move to Ricanau Moffo 21
Chapter 6	Leaving Ricanau Moffo 27
Chapter 7	Back in Paramaribo, November 1964 34
Chapter 8	Missionary Team among Indians 37
Chapter 9	Why Always that Waiting? 39
Chapter 10	Starting Life among the Trios 48
Chapter 11	The Move to PËRËRU TËPU, 1966 53
Chapter 12	What We Learned from the Trios 61
Chapter 13	Missionary Trips by and with the Trios 79
Chapter 14	"Write a book!" many said 95
Chapter 15	Our Family 107
Chapter 16	The Inter-Tribal Bible School 113
Chapter 17	Cultural Things 129
Chapter 18	This Is Not Work! 135
Chapter 19	Hunting and Fishing 139
Chapter 20	Visitors in the Indian Villages 144
Chapter 21	More Outreach 148
Chapter 22	Going! A Sacrifice? 153

Forewords

Although I don't recall the date, I well remember the very first time I met Fred. It was at an evangelistic service in The Netherlands. My wife and I were brand-new missionaries there in the early fifties. We had arranged for an American team to join us for some weeks of meetings and we were right in the middle of the outreach.

On this occasion we were in a church hall doing a meeting for young people. Twelve-year old Fred responded to the invitation and I had the privilege of leading him to Christ at its conclusion. Little did I realize at the time the impact this event would have on so many people in the days ahead.

We kept in touch during part of Fred's teen-age years, but lost contact after we returned to the United States in 1957 and were given a new assignment. But then there came an invitation from the Vermeulens to visit them in Suriname, something I was happy to do on the way back from one of my trips to Uruguay. It was an unforgettable experience for me, never having been in a jungle environment before.

I can still see the Trio elders seated in the church service, facing the congregation. I remember the tune of one the songs they had composed. I remember the older fellow who leaned on the railing of Fred and Trudy's Indian Room to watch the man he called "the teacher of his teacher" eating his lunch. I remember seeing Artwin and a little Trio boy running down the hill hand in hand and jumping into the river together, and Fred's remark about the privileged childhood his kids enjoyed.

This trip was the first of four over a period of a good many years, each one a learning experience for me, noting the respect and admiration the Trios had for Fred and Trudy, for their gracious and loving care and protection for the Vermeulens as well as for me. I'll never forget the thrill of bringing along copies of the newly translated book of Proverbs and how moved I was when the Trios received it as more of *God's Paper* from which I was privileged to teach for the week.

It was easy to understand why Fred and Trudy were anxious to return to Suriname after the vitally important hiatus in Europe to meet their children's needs. I shall always be grateful that our gracious God arranged for our mission in general, and me in particular, to have a small part in the amazing and exciting and fruitful ministries Fred and Trudy faithfully carried on in Suriname.

Henry J Heijermans
General Director Emeritus
WEF Ministries / Biblical Ministries Worldwide

* * * * * * *

"And they sang a new song, saying "Worthy are You to take the book and to break its seals; for You were slain, and purchased for God with Your blood men from every tribe and tongue and people and nation."
Rev. 5:9

I have had the extraordinary privilege of knowing Fred and Trudy Vermeulen for over thirty years. I have enjoyed and benefitted from that friendship both because the Vermeulens are faithful servants of God and because that friendship has afforded me, my wife Marilyn, and members of the congregation, the opportunity to share in ministry with them and to thus witness, first hand, the work of God in the lives of the Indians of Suriname — a work that, in its transformation, is amazing to us but entirely consistent with both the heart and ability of God.

Contained within the pages of this book is the record of God using two ordinary people to deliver people from several tribes from the torment of evil spirits and fear into a relationship with God through Jesus Christ and the subsequent change which that relationship has wrought. The accounts are thrilling and inspiring and will bless all who read them. They will also inspire as well as challenge us to pray for our Indian brothers and sisters in Suriname as they aggressively pursue efforts to share the gospel and their new-found joy and life in Christ with others. They are dear brothers and sisters in Christ, fellow recipients of the grace of God, with whom we will one day have the privilege of joining, along with those of every tribe, tongue, and nation in praise and worship of God. What a day that will be! To God be the glory now and forevermore!

Pastor Marvin Hintz, Delaware OH.

* * * * * * *

Going . . . ! A Sacrifice?

The Bible teaches that one is known by his "fruit." Fred and Trudy are known as 21st century heroes of the faith. Since 1973 Oxford Valley Chapel has been privileged to be their sending church. Over the decades we have seen God use Fred and Trudy beyond our expectations. Additionally, they are both sterling in character and conviction and have glorified our Savior.

Over these many years the Oxford Valley Chapel family has greatly esteemed them as modern day heroes of the faith because of:

- Their love for God and the Gospel
- Their love for each other
- Their steadfast devotion to translating the Bible into the Trio language
- Their unwavering commitment to the work while facing physical, financial, linguistic, and governmental trials
- Their efforts in establishing and equipping the body of Christ in Suriname and beyond
- Their constant servant-leader mindset
- Their godly demeanor and infectious humor

On a personal note, my life has been enriched by serving alongside them in Suriname on two different occasions where I witnessed their love for God, for each other, and for the churches they were serving. My wife (Robin) and I love having them in our home when they are in the area. They enrich our home with their presence!

We are honored to have a small part in their continuing ministry through this book. For those who have not had the opportunity to spend time with Fred and Trudy this book is an opportunity to read how God used these two humble servants for His honor and glory.

It is my desire that this book will encourage others to follow in their footsteps for the fields are still white unto harvest.

Dan Skogen, pastor
Oxford Valley Chapel
Levittown, PA.

* * * * * * *

As the editor of this volume, I have had the privilege of enjoying and being inspired by this memoir, written by faithful servants of the Lord, Fred and Trudy Vermeulen. I met the Vermeulens in the 1980's, when they visited Evangelical

Community Church in Bloomington, Indiana, which supported them for many years. I was impressed by their stories of reaching the Bible Camp site, of gaining a degree of fluency in the Trio language in only six weeks, and of their other work in Suriname, faithfully doing their part in assuring that someday people from "every tribe and nation" will be around the throne of God. Over the years, I have continued to learn about their work through their newsletters.

My parents were medical missionaries in south India; they did not regard their service as sacrifice, either. Like the Vermeulens, sometimes they wished they were closer to loved ones. In those days, plane travel was considered too expensive for missionaries, so my parents were unable to attend my wedding or that of three of my other siblings. They were not able to come to the United States, either, when my older brother was seriously ill, while he was in medical school, or when my mother's father died. Nevertheless, they regarded their experiences and their friendship with colleagues and others in India as a rare privilege, and a reasonable part of their service to the Lord. They helped me and my brothers and sister to look at our experiences, even being away from home in boarding school, in a similarly positive manner.

Like the Vermeulens, my parents were interested in "working themselves out of a job" – training Indian colleagues to take on positions of leadership. It is clear from this memoir that the Vermeulens were successful in training church leaders in Suriname, teaching them from "God's Paper," and encouraging them not only to nurture the people in their congregations and at the Bible Camps but to share the Gospel with people in other tribes, and even in other countries.

Ellie Carman MacDonald
Bloomington, Indiana

Acknowledgements

"Let us not be weary in well-doing: for in due season we shall reap, if we faint not!" Galatians 6:9

Our 'going' to different countries for missionary service is the result, in the first place, of the Lord Jesus Christ, who stepped into our lives. He died, was buried and rose again. The message of His saving grace was brought by Henry and Cathy Heijermans, who left the USA to come to the Netherlands. They arrived in the early 1950's, sent by American churches. Some of those same churches also started supporting us, after our first eight years of missionary work in Suriname, 1964-1972. Other churches joined in supporting us, bringing the total number to twenty. Interestingly enough, there were also twenty individuals and families who faithfully sent in their contributions. We are grateful to all who gave and to all who prayed. All of that happened while serving in Europe, from 1973 to 1992.

Another word of gratefulness goes to those who came to Europe after WWII, to teach Europeans. Many had seen the spiritual condition on that continent, while in the military. They started the Bible Institutes and provided the opportunities for us and many others to prepare for ministry in Europe and across the world. We owe a debt to all these individuals and their sending churches. Our prayer has always been that they will feel a part of what the Lord has been doing.

We are also grateful for those who wrote a foreword for this book and a dear mission-minded lady, who did the editing of these stories. They represent so many others who have stood behind us for so many years.

We are forever grateful to HIM who saved and sent us, and who saw fit to use us all these years. As we have been challenged to serve HIM, may many be challenged by reading these chapters, to consider future missionary service.

ATLANTIC OCEAN
Paramaribo
Ricanau Moffo
Moengo
GUYANA
FRENCH-
GUYANA
SURINAME
stoelmans Isl.
Apetina
Paloemeu
Kawemhakan
Weejo
Oelemarie
RIVER
Tepoe
Känepaku
GUYANA
Litani.River
Alalapodoe
APALAI-area
BRAZIL

Chapter 1

Ministering in Different Places

<u>Overview of our ministries</u>

After more than fifty-four years of ministry, we want to share our experiences with all those who may have an interest in missions, but we hope also to encourage those who at this point have not even thought about being involved in missions, either for a lifetime ministry or perhaps for short-term involvement in foreign missions.

Elsewhere in this book we will share our personal backgrounds, testimonies, and family stories. We will limit ourselves in this book mainly to our years among the Indians in the south of Suriname, but we will also tell you briefly about the other places where we had the privilege of serving.

After the years in Suriname, from 1964-1972, we went back to Europe and in 1973 began a French-speaking ministry in the country and city of Luxembourg. We started services in our living room, with nine adults and seven children. Sunday school was held in our garage. When we began to outgrow our living room, we found a location where we could seat about sixty people, but only forty-two were able to see the speaker. We also had a small room for the Sunday school.

Easter Sunday 1975 we started an English-speaking ministry. Again we were nine adults and seven children. But before the end of that year, we had outgrown those facilities, too, and we moved to a new location, which has been used for many years.

In December 1979 we were asked to be present at a Bible conference in the Trio village of Tepoe in Suriname, which we had left in April 1972. Our colleague, Claude Leavitt, had finished the translation of the New Testament, which was started in the 1960's; we ourselves had translated portions, as we needed them for teaching. At the same time Ivan and Doris Schoen had finished the translation of the Wayana New Testament.

After receiving their copies of the New Testament, the Indians asked us to return to minister to them again. "Now we have God's Paper, but nobody to teach us. We don't want to be like a tribe in Brazil, who after they received God's Paper, there was nobody to teach them. Therefore they started dancing in a circle, around God's Paper!" they told us.

In 1979 our mission asked us to move to Germany and take an administrative position, which after some time turned out to be for all the countries in Europe, where workers in our mission were doing church planting. The name of that mission at that time was Worldwide European Fellowship but, after a merger with United Missionary Fellowship in the 1980's, the name was changed to Biblical Ministries Worldwide.

We were given permission by our mission board to return to Suriname on an annual basis for six weeks. This is what we were able to do until the spring of 1986. Shortly thereafter, fighting started on the coast of Suriname and spread to the interior of the country; Indians were enlisted by both sides in the conflict.

It was summer 1986 when we were asked to go to Maastricht, in the Netherlands. The church there was started by one of the Biblical Ministries Worldwide missionaries. Our assignment was to help the church get back on its feet, after a sad experience they had had with their first national pastor. We went there and after six years, in 1992, when the attendance had gone up from about twenty to close to one hundred, the church split.

About that same time the ministry in the country of Suriname opened up again for us. In consultation with the pastors of at least six of our supporting churches, we were encouraged by each one of them to return to that tribal ministry. For health reasons, we were not able to live in the jungle full-time again, but we went to Suriname several times per year from then on. The original goal was Bible teaching, but in November 1993 it became obvious that we needed to continue translating the Old Testament, as our colleague Claude was not able to do translation any longer. A few years later we also started the Inter-tribal Bible School, about which you can read elsewhere in this book.

"Let us go over unto the other side of the lake!" Luke 8:22

Chapter 2

God's Leading to Suriname, 1960

In January 1959 I started my Bible training in France. The strategic location of the European Bible Institute, near Paris and its airports, offered many traveling missionaries, pastors, and mission leaders the opportunity to visit the school, sometimes just for short visits. It was great to hear the challenges by these preachers. The only thing that I did not enjoy at the time was the questions they would ask at the table, at noon or at suppertime. "Where are you from?" "How did you come to EBI?" "What year are you in?" "Where do you plan to serve the Lord?"

Many of the students already had a clear idea of where they were going to serve the Lord, but I did not know at that time. Missions in some primitive country? Probably!

The loss of life by five missionaries in Ecuador in 1956, had made quite an impression on both Trudy and me, although we had not met yet when that happened. It spoke to our hearts and it challenged us, while neither one of us was suicidal!

Students shared rooms in a big old French building in one of the suburbs of Paris. The rooms housed four students, or six or eight or even more. I spent my first semester in a room that held eight students, all in the French department. A good opportunity to learn real French! All I knew was school French, which I had learned during six years in elementary school and high school.

Since I liked to get up early, I was appointed to light the gas heater. It was turned off every night, and lit again every morning. The first time was a disaster. The gas accumulated after the pressure of it had extinguished the match. Quickly I lit a new match and put it through the small opening in the heater. The result was a loud explosion. The lid flew off the stove and dust, which had accumulated over a number of years — after all, it was a boys' room — flew all over the room.

The explosion woke up not only the fellows in my room, but also the students in the neighboring room. One of them had come in after the lights had been turned off, the night before. He had thrown his white shirt over one of the chairs and gone to bed. When he woke up from this terrific noise, he jumped out of bed, and since he did not have his glasses on, he could only see something white, and was convinced that the ceiling had fallen down. Panic! But after he found his glasses, he saw that it was just his white shirt and not part of the ceiling.

My second semester I was assigned to a room housing four students. Believe me, it was quite an interesting team, from different countries! One of my roommates was a Greek pastor, who had come to learn more about the Bible. His previous schooling had consisted of Greek Orthodox doctrine. He was a very serious man, who firmly believed that Christians were not supposed to have fun or laugh.

We had two bunk beds in the room and he slept on one of the bottom bunks. Every evening the lights in the whole building were supposed to be turned off at ten o'clock sharp. The signal for lights-out was a bell ringing. That was the responsibility of one of the students who slept on the upper bunk, above the Greek man, who always got into his bed a few minutes before ten, and lay straight on his back, with his eyes closed. One evening we put a wet sponge, underneath the top mattress and wrapped it in plastic. When the student came back from ringing the bell, he always had to get into bed in the dark. When he did it that night, some water was squeezed out of the sponge and fell on the Greek pastor's face. A scream followed, so the light had to be turned on again. Everyone was in bed and our roommate had no idea of who had thrown water on him. When the person above him got into bed the second time, the same thing happened again. Again the lights were turned on, but he was not able to determine who had thrown the water on him. He did not find out until the next morning at the breakfast table. With all the students present, the practical joke was explained to him. At the time, he didn't think it was funny at all. But over the course of the months that followed, he developed a sense of humor, too.

The president of the Student Missionary Fellowship was also in our room that semester. He was John Dewerse, from Belgium. One day he gave me a letter from a pastor in Suriname and said: "Is this something for you?" The pastor had sent this letter to the student body, explaining the need for workers in that country. Actually, he needed help right away and was wondering if anybody would be available. It sure looked interesting. It was the type of ministry which appealed to me.

Suriname was still one of the colonies of the Netherlands. Dutch was the official language and ministry was possible in several languages. About fifteen languages are spoken in that country, with a population of half a million. I wondered whether I should write to the pastor.

I returned the letter to John and tried to put it out of my mind. Just doing something because of all those visiting preachers and missionaries, who were constantly putting you on the spot, was not a reason to write.

From time to time the need in Suriname came back to my mind. Finally I wrote a letter and asked this pastor for more information. That was the beginning of an intensive correspondence. But when this pastor started writing as if I and my future wife Trudy were already on our way to Suriname, and indicated that he was counting on us, I brought the correspondence to a sudden halt. Was this God's will or the will of man?

That is when I decided to stop answering those letters from Suriname.

It was now a matter of seeking the Lord's mind. I turned to God and his Word and asked Him to give me a clear answer from His Word, as I systematically began reading the Bible. I was looking for His will in His Word. I don't know whether it was days later, or maybe a few weeks later, when I came across a passage in Luke, chapter eight, that spoke to my dilemma. It tells the story of Jesus and His disciples in a boat on a lake. Somebody had spoken on those verses in chapel not too long before. The question which Jesus had asked of His disciples was a very interesting one:

'Where is your faith?'

What did the disciples have to have faith in? What had Jesus said to his disciples? As I thought about those verses, it became clear to me that Jesus had given His disciples instructions and that He had set His goal: Go over to the other side of the sea!

For me, it was not the idea of going over to the other side, the crossing of the ocean from Europe to Suriname, that impressed me, but the definite goal Jesus had set. It was not something vague or uncertain, not going out on the sea. Not finding a place to rest for some time. The goal was: to go over to the other side! The disciples had not shown faith in these words of Jesus. They were afraid of perishing in the sea, with the storm keeping them from reaching the other side. Thinking about this passage brought calm to the storm in my mind.

I started up the correspondence again. Questions and answers were sent by mail, in both directions. When Trudy and I talked about these things, during the few times every year that we saw each other, while I was in Bible training in France and she was in nurses' training in the Netherlands, we experienced peace and joy and a oneness in heart and mind that comes when following God's plan for one's life.

After graduating from the European Bible Institute, in June 1962, I went to England, where I began my linguistics training close to London. The courses were given at the Summer Institute of Linguistics, or SIL, as everybody knew it. The buildings of a former military camp were used.

Trudy had, earlier that year, received her official papers as a Registered Nurse, but was still finishing some courses in midwifery. My plan was to take some training at the Missionary School for Medicine in London after finishing the SIL course. My suitcases with clothes and other personal belongings were at the school already. After Trudy received her diploma in midwifery, she too came over to England, to help with the cooking at SIL. Her plan was to find a place in a hospital in London, in order to gain more experience and additional training in the medical realm, while I planned to study tropical medicine.

However, during the last weeks at SIL, Trudy's and my plans began to change. The classes were not only profitable for learning a new language and reducing unwritten languages to writing, but gave much insight into missionary life and different cultures.

One lesson that we learned from one of the anthropologists at SIL was a lesson which would be of much help later and in several different countries. She mentioned that no matter where we would go as missionaries, we would discover that the people to whom we were going to minister would not be different. "You missionaries are going to be different!" she said. Soon we would discover how valuable that insight was going to be in our ministry in various places.

After eight years in Suriname, the Lord's path brought us to ministries in a number of European countries. We had heard about 'culture shock' from our colleagues in Suriname, but did not know what it was. They explained it to us. Returning to the Netherlands for six years in 1986, after having been away for twenty-eight years, we experienced culture shock ourselves.

Another teaching guest, who had spent considerable time on mission fields himself, spoke about the danger of getting too involved in social work, at the expense of one's spiritual ministry. That opened my eyes. My desire was to share the Word of God with people who had not yet heard, so getting involved in other things could be a danger. Fortunately, Trudy had plenty of training in the medical realm, to do the necessary things to help people in a tribe.

Soon thereafter we shared these changes in our plans with Trudy's mother and my parents. My parents had paid for all my studies, as they had done for my three brothers and three sisters. By the end of September 1962, we were back in the Netherlands, where both of us found jobs and made plans for a wedding. November 14th was chosen for that occasion. Although the pastor in Suriname began to finalize plans for our arrival in Suriname, things did not go as quickly as everyone had expected. There was still God's plan, and we had to wait for God's timing.

I had found a job at the Netherlands Railroad Headquarters. It was office work, one thing I had always detested doing. But as both of us would experience again later: Do not ever say 'Never' to God.

There were things to learn in that office which later proved to be very useful. There was much opportunity to live for the Lord among those seventeen workers in that big room, but also in other rooms connected with that one. Those fourteen months turned out to be very valuable.

The fact that my work in the office had been appreciated was not only mentioned by my boss, at the end of these fourteen months. More than one year later we received an additional sum of money from this employer, citing the amount of work I had done while working there.

Trudy had no problem either in finding work, as a nurse and midwife. Sometimes she worked for short periods of time in hospitals and sometimes for longer periods in private homes, caring for terminal patients or assisting in deliveries in homes. Taking care of mothers and their new babies was what she enjoyed most.

On October 4, 1963 our first baby was born, Rosyanne Chanita. The arrival of our daughter delayed our departure for Suriname still further. The shipping company did not allow a pregnant woman to travel with them, after a certain number of months of pregnancy. Departure was finally scheduled for January 15th, 1964, from Amsterdam to Paramaribo, by way of Hamburg, Germany. It was a very cold trip, because it was one of the coldest winters that part of Europe had known in years. There were icebreakers in the port of Hamburg twenty-four hours per day. It was even so cold that the cabins on our ship could not be properly heated. Probably the only passenger on board who did not suffer from the low temperatures was Rosyanne. Even when we passed the Azores it was too cold to go on deck. But who would care to be on deck while being seasick? And during the days when we felt good enough to be up, there was work to do: cutting and sorting all the flannelgraph figures for teaching Bible stories to people in Suriname.

"Wait on the Lord, and keep His way, and He shall exalt thee to inherit the land! Psalm 37:34 a

Chapter 3

In Paramaribo

We arrived in Suriname on January 30, 1964. It took us fourteen days to go from Amsterdam to Paramaribo on S.S. Chiron, one of the ships of the KNSM, the Royal Netherlands Steamship Company. We went by way of Hamburg, Germany to pick up additional cargo for Suriname. Trudy and I just had a couple of crates, plus our rattan chairs. In order to save us some money, the captain of the ship allowed us to put our chairs on deck. That way we would not have to pay for their shipping. Paying for all that bulk would have deterred us from even taking them. There were six cabins, each one designed for two people. Rosyanne was the thirteenth passenger. She slept in a big basket, which the company provided. It was so good to have finally passed the Gulf of Biscay. That was the end of the rough weather, or so we thought. But one of the officers informed us that our seasickness would soon return, as we would be finding ourselves in a different current. He was a professional, and of course he was right!

The next day, nobody showed up for breakfast. At certain times, during certain days, we all felt better and walked around a little bit, and worked on our flannelgraph.

It was so good to finally be told that the next day we would be arriving in Paramaribo! All of us were excited, even the two nuns who were on board, on their way to a term of service in one of the Suriname schools. How joyful they had been just before we left Amsterdam. The news that one of the members of the Dutch Royal Family had converted to Roman Catholicism, was the reason for that joy. The whole royal family belonged to the Dutch Reformed Church.

We approached the port of Paramaribo shortly after three o'clock in the morning, while it was still dark. The ship remained in the middle of the muddy Suriname River. There was no room for us to dock. It seemed to take forever for the sky to get light that day; about five-thirty was the normal time. But it was much later when we were asked to leave the ship and get into a smaller boat, which would take us to the offices of immigration and customs. By the time we were met by our superintendent, the sun was shining in all its glory and produced welcome heat. We were welcomed by our mission leader in the country, whom we had met for the first time in London, while in linguistic training. He knew people in immigration and got us out of those buildings in a very short time.

We will probably never forget our first impression of the city of Paramaribo. With our European background, everything looked very poor and neglected. We could imagine that the beautiful colonial style buildings had adorned this city in years gone by. Now many buildings needed paint and the streets needed cleaning. We were taken to our house, behind a girls' school. The house was completely furnished and the furniture was made of beautiful Suriname wood. All the windows had screens and right away we noticed the mosquito netting above our bed. We were pleasantly surprised with our accommodations!

One thing we could not initially agree with was the instruction that we were given that first day, to rest every afternoon. We were not told to sleep, but to retire to our bed. Within just a few days we began to see the necessity of this instruction. Schools closed at one o'clock and so did the stores and all government offices. Actually, it was very quiet on the streets between two and four in the afternoons, but the temperature was high. We were in the tropics!

Our introduction to the different activities of our superintendent began the next day. First of all, we were shown much of the girls' school. Then we were taken to the small church building on Keizerstraat.

The different schools in the district were next on the agenda.

Several days later we were introduced to Mrs. Sprang, a very kind Surinamese lady, who spoke the Suriname language, called Sranang Tongo, as well as Dutch and English. She helped us to learn Sranang Tongo – a kind of pigeon English, a mixture of English and Dutch. That trade language is also called Takki-takki. (Do you get it? Talk-talk!)

The following Sunday we were taken to the church service and met all the members of the English-speaking congregation. A week later we met the members of the Dutch-speaking congregation. Some of the people were the same as the previous week. We also were given a welcoming service, which was held in the Stads-Zending – a beautiful building, belonging to the Moravian

Church, called Evangelische Broeder Gemeente. These churches are the result of active missionary work, a long time ago. Count Zinzendorf was the one who was the founder of all this missionary work. The other name that was used for this ministry is Herrnhut. Some of the other Dutch and American missionaries were present. All were from other mission organizations.

We saw much of the city, during the various rides with our superintendent. All the government buildings looked beautiful and so did the palace of the governor. But we had not come for sightseeing. We wanted to be involved in ministry.

Very soon those opportunities were offered to us. Not only was I invited to speak, in both English and Dutch services, but we started holding meetings in one of the schools in the district, on Saturday nights. These meetings were supposed to be evangelistic in nature and many attended, especially young people, who loved to sing gospel songs. It was humorous to hear our superintendent preach messages on Sunday morning that I had prepared and preached the night before!

There were also radio programs on different stations. Many different churches provided programs for certain days, or certain weeks on three different stations. Sometimes those programs lasted only 10-15 minutes; they were often broadcasted early in the morning, when people were ready to go to work. Other programs were fifteen or thirty minutes long, during the morning hours, a little later. So often we met people, in stores or on the streets, who recognized my voice from these radio programs. Even later on while we were situated in the jungle, we had the opportunity to provide tapes with a Bible message. We were surprised that a number of the participating pastors either forgot their turn, or at times did not want to bother preparing and recording a message. In speaking with the management of those stations we found out that all of them were very anxious to get extra tapes from us, so they could put them on the air whenever someone else did not provide a program.

It was not always easy to get a program ready for exactly the number of minutes allowed by the radio station. We had to do the entire recording ourselves, even some music at the beginning and the closing of the message.

Although we were not yet on our mission post, there were plenty of opportunities to minister. Was there fruit from the sowing of that seed?

But my God shall supply all your need according to His riches in glory by Christ Jesus. Philippians 4:19

Chapter 4

Visits to Ricanau Moffo

After arriving in Suriname on January 30, 1964 we were soon taken to the Aucaner village of Ricanau Moffo on the Cottica River. That was going to be our base of operations, with the possibility of working in other villages, where some missionary work had been done before. There was already a school right next to the village, with a young lady teaching all the different grades in one room.

Meeting with the village leaders at Ricanau Moffo

Our superintendent informed us that we would have to meet officially with all the village leaders, the so-called Captain and the so-called bashas. The bashas are under the Captain. Somewhere in a village downriver was the Chief of the tribe, called Granman. Most of these officials were involved in witchcraft, in various degrees. We presume that they had consulted with the spirits about our coming. They probably did not have the power to keep us from coming to minister the Word of God so close to the village. After all, it was not their territory. But they could certainly give us all kinds of opposition. On our first visit we were taken to the offering place in the village and were even allowed to take pictures. That meeting was not to decide whether we would be allowed to move to the mission station or not. It was more like a general and official welcome to the area.

We were also told that it was the custom to provide the drink for this meeting - either the quite strong drink, called sopy, or regular soft drinks. We gave no consideration to the first possibility. We were not going to contribute to the problem of drunkenness that already existed in the villages. Some of the young men regularly went to French Guyana to buy alcohol and smuggled it across the border into Suriname. Much later, some of them told us that more than once they had been caught and lost both the drink they had bought and the money they had invested in it.

We were going to be taken by car to Moengo by our superintendent. The Captain would pick us up and take us downriver to the village of Ricanau Moffo. It was going to be the beginning of our official move from the city to the interior to begin our ministry.

In Paramaribo we bought a crate of soft drinks, produced locally. We still had no idea how the soft drinks were going to be used, except that people would drink them. We would find out quickly after our meeting started. Everyone was given a bottle, after someone had opened all the bottles. Then the meeting started. The village leaders, both men and women, each took their turn in welcoming us personally and then proceeded to address the other leaders, rather than us.

When the first leader started, we noticed that he wiped off the top of the bottle and then poured some of the drink on the ground in front of him. Nothing special about that, we thought. He probably had some rust from the cap on the bottle. But as he talked, he would drink a little and then pour some on the ground in front of him. He certainly gave us the impression that there was lots of rust in his drink. Or maybe he was showing us his dissatisfaction with the soft drink and wanted to make it clear to us that he would have preferred the really strong drink.

But when the second person and the third person did exactly the same thing, we began to wonder about this procedure. By that time it was the turn for the man closest to us to do the talking. As he poured some drink on the clay ground in front of him, we noticed that a bottle had been buried in the clay, upside down. Now it was clear what they were doing. We had been told that bottles were used as a dwelling place for the spirits. We had seen them by the huts and also around the place where offerings were made to the spirits. Then, looking around the circle, we could easily see that there was a bottle buried in the ground in front of each one in attendance, even in front of us. The small stools on which we were sitting had been placed exactly in front of a bottle.

"Lord! Is this the way we must begin our ministry?" I prayed. "Do not allow this to continue, God!"

And as soon as I had silently prayed this way, this part of the ceremony stopped. All the others in the circle did their talking, but there was no more pouring of soft drink. It was the first victory through prayer.

Thus ended our first meeting with the leaders of the village and the other inhabitants.

Back in Paramaribo we looked at different possibilities for purchasing materials to build our house in Ricanau Moffo. One possibility was just to buy those materials and take them into the interior. Then we were made aware of the possibility of taking apart an existing building in a leprosy colony. Because new medication had been developed to treat leprosy patients, the colony was no longer needed to the same extent. Most of the buildings had already been abandoned. Then, for some reason, we were led to the Bruynzeel Lumber Company. They were producing building materials and even building different types of houses in and around the city of Paramaribo. When we visited their offices, we were introduced to a Dutchman from the province of Limburg in Holland, Jack van der Berg. We hit it off right away, as he was very anxious to speak the dialect of that province with me, since I was born in that same province. We looked at the different models that Bruynzeel was building in those days. We felt that one model suited us best. It had a living room and 3 small bedrooms. Jack, of course, was interested in selling us that type of house, but then he asked us how we would pay for it. When he heard that we did not even have the down payment for it, he asked us how much money we would be able to afford per month. Well, we could not even answer that question.

We eventually decided on Sf 100 per month, which was the equivalent of approximately US $50. At that point we had no idea how we would come up with that amount. But we knew we would have to trust the Lord in that matter and in much more. Now the problem was to buy all the extras, like cement and cement blocks for the pillars of the house (stilts), a kitchen sink and a shower, all the windows with screens, and all the paint. It seemed best to paint both the inside and the outside of the house and we were advised also to paint the roof. It would be made of galvanized sheets and, because of the quality we had ordered, would probably rust quickly.

Step by step, we saw God work out the details of the decision of this purchase. At the end of the morning everything that was needed to build our home in Ricanau Moffo was on the invoice. The monthly amount we had to pay remained the same. Two southerners — from the south of the Netherlands— had struck a deal, which, we are sure, was a better deal for us than it was for the Bruynzeel Company.

Now we needed to transport all these materials to the village of Ricanau Moffo. They could go by road, the East-West connector. But the road went only as far as Moengo, which is half an hour upstream from Ricanau Moffo on the Cottica River. Moengo had a large bauxite plant and even large bauxite ships went there. Most of the supplies for that part of the country went by smaller boats. There was even a small freight boat that traveled from Paramaribo to Moengo once a week with lots of supplies, but the owner had a full load each week. However, he was willing to make an extra trip with our building materials and more supplies for the stores.

So, soon after our purchase, everything was loaded on his boat and I left Paramaribo one late afternoon, going down the Suriname River and then up the Cottica River.

I slept, or should I say spent the night, on the deck of that boat, and we arrived early the next morning at the mouth of the Ricanau Creek, where the village was located. Ricanau Moffo means the mouth (Moffo) of the Ricanau. That is where the creek flows into the Cottica River.

Walter, who was the government-appointed Captain of the village, had arranged with a number of the young men to unload the boat. It took them all morning.

By the time we completed the purchase of all the lumber and the rest of the building materials and arranged for the transport of all of it, we had also located two men from French Guyana who were both doing carpentry work in Paramaribo. One of them had already built some beautiful bookcases for us from the boards of our crates. They both had experience in building homes and were willing to spend time in the interior to build our home. The price of building had already been fixed, so we could be sure that they would not be wasting their time, or ours.

Soon after our arrival, the work started. Trudy and I had picked the spot for our house already and so that same day we did some more measuring and we started digging the foundation. Late that afternoon Captain Walter took me back to Moengo, where I got on one of those 'wild buses' which functioned as taxis. At that stage of the game, there wasn't much I could do. There were still things to do in Paramaribo in one of the small churches there and we needed to work on other preparations for living in Ricanau Moffo.

Within two weeks I went back to check up on how things were going with the work on the house. It was encouraging to see how much progress had been made already. The agreement with the two workers, which was that they would receive some money when they started on the job, so they could buy supplies for themselves, and the rest of the amount upon completing the building, proved to have been a very good decision. They had worked very hard and continued to do so after I left.

I did spend several days with them. One of the first things they shared with me was their unusual experience after dark. During the nights they had heard strange sounds, like the boards and planks being picked up and moved. When I asked them if they had missed any materials, they told me that they had not. If they had said that materials were missing, I would have been very suspicious. While still in the city, they had told me about their past – they had both been in prison for various reasons — but they claimed that they had made a new start in life and wanted to make an honest living. We knew already that none of the villagers would ever come to the mission station after dark. They would not come on the trail, nor by river. All the villagers were very much afraid of the evil spirits, which, they claimed, live in the tops of the trees and bushes. For that reason everyone left the station just before dark, to make it back to the village, which was only a ten-minute walk for them, over a trail which took them only through second growth. We knew that they would never come to the station by canoe, after dark, with bad intentions either. Everything in front of the school and our new house was too open.

That evening I went to sleep on my cot, protected by my mosquito-netting, not mainly to protect me from those biting insects, but to protect me from the many bats, which started to show up just before dark. Then I had done what I had been advised by these two men, and that was to put my cot on top of some school benches, to protect us from the many rats that showed up every night looking for food in the classroom.

I do not remember how long I had been awake, listening to all the different noises of the jungle: crickets and birds, monkeys in the distance, the mosquitoes buzzing around the netting and the first snoring of my French-speaking roommates. I do not remember either how long I had slept before waking up and hearing some strange noises. Those were the noises these two men had heard and which they had told me about. It was only for a few moments that it bothered me.

I quickly sent my petitions up to God, telling Him that we wanted to serve Him there to overcome the powers of darkness in His power.

Was I surprised by the fact that the sounds disappeared so quickly, and that I didn't hear them anymore? Not that night or in the nights to come. When I woke up that morning, I was eager to find out if any material was missing or had been moved. And that was certainly not the case! After several days I returned to Paramaribo, and Trudy and I began to make plans to move from the city to our new place of ministry.

"How shall they call on Him..?" Romans 10:14

Chapter 5

Move to Ricanau Moffo

In early May 1964 Trudy and I, with our 8-month-old daughter Rosyanne, left Paramaribo to begin our ministry among the Aucaner people on the Cottica River. Many of the villagers spent much of the first day with us but, just before dark, everyone disappeared over the narrow trail through the jungle, back to their village. The different sounds were there again, as well as the noises from the village. We turned on our kerosene lanterns and began to notice the hundreds of mosquitoes buzzing outside our screened window. It was quite a choir, but the sound was very monotonous. The first few nights we slept very well and woke up only when it started to get light again, but then we began to hear different noises above our heads each night. Scores of bats had found housing between the galvanized roof and our ceiling. The pieces of board, which had been cut in the shape of the corrugated sheets of galvanized roofing and the rafters, did not prevent the bats from entering and spending the days there and part of the nights. Soon the young bats began to find their way on top of the ceiling boards, and they kept us from getting a good night's rest.

One of the young women was very anxious to help Trudy with various things that had to be done in the house. I spent the days in painting both the inside and outside of the house. Quite a few men, including the Captain of the village, proved to be very willing helpers in the task of digging a hole for the septic tank. When we asked for helpers to open up more area around the house and school, they showed up early in the morning to start the work. All they were asking for as pay was about two dollars and fifty cents per day. It gave us a good opportunity to get to know them better.

Trudy started painting on the inside of the house, but had to keep an eye on Rosyanne as well. When Rosyanne was remarkably quiet, she went to check on her. "OH, NO!" She had found our wedding picture album and decided that the pictures needed to be removed from those pages.

Very soon thereafter, we began having a service in the school building every Sunday morning. Not knowing enough of their language, I had to ask the schoolteacher for help in interpreting for me. The men knew most of the songs in a Dutch hymnbook. Trudy played the guitar. Trudy and I both did all we could to learn their language which, with our Dutch background and knowledge of English, was not too hard. Within a few weeks we were able to gently tell the schoolteacher that we wanted to start doing the services by ourselves.

In the first few weeks we were not sure whether the schoolteacher was saved or not, but soon it became obvious that, while she knew much about Christianity and the Bible, she had never made a personal decision for Christ, nor did our times of sharing and talking with her lead to her making that decision during our stay there. Later on, we heard that not only she, but also our neighbor, who owned a store right next to the mission station, came to personal faith in Christ. After we had let that teacher know that we were not going to need her help in interpreting, there seemed to be quite a distance between her and us.

Although no girls attended the school, they did attend the services. Previous experiences with male schoolteachers had made the village leaders decide not to allow the girls to attend school any longer. Some of the girls had become pregnant by one or more of the teachers.

That is also the reason why the decision was made to send a female teacher to the village.

Attendance in the services was good. Both young men and women started coming and the Lord began to give much liberty in teaching His Word. What a joy it was when about six of the young men expressed their desire to trust Christ and become born again. Such fruit in such a short time! What else could we expect? We soon found out what was in store for us.

Our superintendent sent us a letter, telling us that he was planning to visit us with one of the ladies from the English-speaking congregation in Paramaribo, Sister Sprang.

She and her husband had spent some time among these people and she wanted to come back for a visit.

Trudy and I looked forward to this visit and to sharing with them what God was doing. We had been put in charge of developing and supervising the ministry on the Cottica River. Some additional information and advice from our superintendent would certainly be welcome. He had told us that we had complete freedom to go about our ministry and that he had no intention of being involved in it. After all, he was involved in so many things in the city. He had two small congregations in the city, one English-speaking and one Dutch-speaking. He was also involved in the school, where hundreds of girls learned homemaking skills: cooking, sewing, cleaning and much more. In addition, he was supervising several elementary schools with hundreds of children just outside the city, in the district. In the evenings he taught in a high school. No wonder he had been asking for someone to take over the work in the interior!

We picked up both this pastor and Mrs. S. in the town of Moengo.

First of all, we took them to visit the mission station and the school. Both were very impressed with all the changes and improvements. Then we proceeded to the village to meet with the leaders there.

New things were brought to our attention, which would certainly be helpful in understanding more of the culture and the different villagers.

After spending time with the Captain and the villagers, we returned to the mission station via that narrow path through the jungle. Once we were back in our home again, we discussed the ministry and our plans. At that time we began to have questions about our superintendent and his beliefs and practices. For one thing, we were asked to teach catechism in the school every week. Then he told us that after we had done that for a few months, he would come back to baptize those boys. Had he not put us in charge of that ministry? Had he not told us to develop that ministry on the whole river? Was that the future of our ministry? It raised many questions and it was the reason for much concern on our part.

We had experienced the first victories for Christ. Were we facing the first attacks from our adversary now?

We took our guests back to Moengo with many questions on our minds. But these reasons for serious concern were followed by a very humorous event. When we finally stopped our speed boat at the riverbank, we needed to move some canoes in order to get close enough to allow our guests to go ashore. Unfortunately Mrs. S. was not willing to wait for me to move those canoes to the right spots. Even when I asked her to wait for me, so that I could come to the front of our boat and move the closest canoe, she continued her efforts to move those canoes herself. Now you should know that she weighed closer to three hundred pounds than two hundred! As she proceeded to lean over to move one canoe, she also managed to get up on the front of our speedboat. Our next plea for patience on her part was ignored as well, and by that time she was pushing so hard on the canoe that it began to move forward. At the same time she was pushing our own boat back. The distance between the two became greater and greater; she finally managed to have both feet on the side of our boat, while holding on to the canoe with both hands.

How can we describe the splashing of water when all those pounds landed, face forward, in the Cottica River? Fortunately, the place where she landed was very shallow. She was able to get up and out of the water. I jumped on shore in just a few seconds and helped her climb the riverbank. Even being that close to her, I did not see her face. And we never saw her face again!

We are told in the Word that we cannot serve two masters. The folks there told us that you should not have your feet in two different canoes! Good illustration!

The visit we had looked forward to had become a very disheartening encounter. Trudy and I talked, thought, prayed, and wondered what the outcome would be. We went to bed with heavy hearts, but the next day we began with new courage and determination. God had brought us there and supplied our needs in wonderful ways. He had provided a new 20 H.P. outboard motor and the money was coming in to pay all our debt, for house and motor, on a monthly basis.

We knew that when there is victory, we must also expect opposition.

So the work continued. The work of improving the station was going well. Contact with the villagers was good and attendance at the services was encouraging.

We realized, however, that we could not let our superintendent think that we had begun teaching catechism in the school. At the same time we wondered about what the mission leaders in the United States were thinking. All we had in writing about that organization was so positive. After several weeks we realized that we needed to write letters to both the leader in Paramaribo and to the leadership in the U.S.

Writing those letters was not the problem. Mailing them was the problem. We did not have the fuel to make another trip to the town of Moengo. Actually mailing these letters could wait till the following week. But the next day we heard someone approaching the village in a motor boat. There weren't all that many motors in the area. As the motor approached the station, we proceeded to the riverside with the letters in hand. Was this boat going to Moengo? If so, nobody would refuse to mail some letters for us. The boat stopped at our dock and we introduced ourselves, at the same time asking if the man was going to Moengo and would be willing to mail the letters for us. The answer was 'yes' to both questions. And when he looked at both envelopes, he exclaimed: "This man in Paramaribo is my uncle and I can give both letters to him! I will be seeing him anyway!" We could not ask him to give the letters back, but we did ask him to just mail the letter going to the United States.

We both had our doubts about our letter carrier, especially when several weeks later we still had no answer, either from our superintendent or from the mission's headquarters. We just continued with our work.

On one of our weekly visits to Moengo we met a lady who was married to a storeowner. We had first met her in the church in the city. She asked some questions about our work and how it was going. For a reason unknown to us, she began talking about our superintendent, who was also the pastor who had performed her wedding ceremony.

Then she shared with us that he was a member of a secret society and that he was quite involved in it.

On the following Sunday morning, when I was having my devotions and doing my final preparations before the service, I experienced a definite uneasiness about the whole situation. Not knowing exactly why, I realized that the end of our ministry among these dear people might be coming to an end. After the service Trudy and I discussed the situation and we decided to make a trip to Paramaribo to meet with our superintendent to let him know that we had decided to resign from the mission.

"Abraham, when he was called…went out,
not knowing whither he went!" Hebrews 11:8

Chapter 6

Leaving Ricanau Moffo

It was on Sunday, November 8, 1964 when it became clear that we would not be able to continue to minister among these people, under the supervision of the superintendent in Paramaribo. We would have had to compromise and had no intention of doing so.

Early the next morning we traveled the 30 minutes by speedboat from Ricanau Moffo to Moengo. We borrowed a car from the Gomperts family. Ruud worked for Alcoa/Suralco in Moengo. We had befriended them and had witnessed to them. They had come to visit us at the station, and we had stayed in their home and had spent many wonderful hours with them. They had also introduced us to some wonderful fruits and foods from Suriname. On one occasion we had stayed one night in their home to be with their son, while they were away. Ellie had prepared a wonderful bowl of mashed papaya fruit and suggested that we put it in the freezer for a little while, because it would taste even better when it was cold. It wasn't until the next morning that we remembered that we had put this great tasting dish in the freezer. When we ate it the next day, it was the most delicious thing we had eaten in a long time. Afterwards, we enjoyed this kind of dessert many more times.

We had been able to use their car a number of times for our shopping in Moengo. That was much easier than walking and carrying groceries and other purchases from the stores to our boat. Some of the stores were up to two miles away from the river. They had told us that we were welcome to use their car to go to Paramaribo and that we didn't need to hurry back, but to stay in the city as long as we needed. Of course, we could have gotten on one of those 'wild buses' again to go to Paramaribo, but then we would have had to use those buses many more times in the city as well. There were a number of things we needed to accomplish on this trip. The main purpose of our going was to inform our superintendent about our resignation.

Once we were in the city, we needed to locate him. Since he was involved in so many things and schools during the day, we would have to visit those places one by one. We did locate him eventually in one of the schools in the district, directly south of Paramaribo.

When we sat down in his simple office, at first he did not give us the impression that he was aware of the reason for our coming to the city. But when we shared with him our concerns and feelings, he made comments that gave us a clear indication that he was prepared for our news. Some accusations followed, which gave us clues that he had read the letter which we had sent to the mission leadership in Pennsylvania. That sealed letter had been given to him by his cousin, whom we had stopped that afternoon, weeks before. The superintendent had obviously opened and read both letters, not just the one addressed to him.

Soon thereafter we discovered that he had told some of his friends about our letter to him. At one point Trudy and I were both afraid that he was going to collapse from a heart attack, especially when he accused us of making our decision based on the fact that we were white and he was black. And black he was. But why would we have come to serve our Lord among these people if we were prejudiced or racially bigoted? When we had been with him in his car, driving around the city, to learn more about the city and the country, we had had interesting experiences. Whenever he saw someone he knew, walking by the wayside or on the sidewalk, he would stop his car and ask that person: "What are you doing here...?" This sounded so strange to us, because of his own very black skin. He would never stop long enough to get an answer, but push the gas pedal and continue on. We know, and the Lord knows, that we had never held racially prejudiced feelings toward him, or toward anyone else.

This very difficult encounter was behind us. Now we needed to inform others in the city about our resignation from that mission. Each one asked us what our plans were. We had no plans, except the determination to stay in the country. The Lord had brought us to Suriname and we were not leaving because of this negative experience. HE would certainly have a different place of ministry for us.

The rest of that day and the several days that followed were filled with wonderful words of encouragement from several sources. A German missionary who had worked in Ricanau Moffo years before shared his thoughts with us. Many others had wondered how we would fare in our ministry and in our affiliation with our superintendent. When we told one missionary that we had no intention of leaving Suriname, he told us that our superintendent would claim back the show-money, which had been paid to the Suriname government by him. He also told us that that process would automatically cancel our visas to stay in the country.

We also spent some time with MAF pilot Roy Parsons and his wife Katie, whom we had gotten to know during the months we spent in Paramaribo, right after our arrival in Suriname, at a reception with the governor of Suriname. Later they came to visit us in Ricanau Moffo, and we even spent some time with their whole family in Albina and St. Laurent, on the other side of the Marowijne River in French Guyana.

Our superintendent had made some negative remarks when we had told him that we had met this couple and that we had spent some time with them, but in those days we had no idea of his reasons for making those comments.

Right away, after informing Roy & Katie about our resignation, they invited us to stay with them, once we had left Ricanau Moffo. "We have our personal support, so we can trust the Lord together to supply the needs for all of us!" they said. That was the first step in the right direction.

Another missionary couple, working upstream from Ricanau Moffo and even Moengo, on the Cottica River, graciously offered us their help with moving our belongings from Ricanau Moffo to Pelgrim Kondre, and storing them there for as long as necessary. All we had was the speedboat, certainly not big enough to transport our things. It would take at least one hour by boat from our station to theirs. But they had a large dugout canoe, able to handle much more than what we had.

How were we going to finance all of this moving and then the return to Paramaribo?

All we had in our bank account was approximately seventeen dollars. That was enough to buy gas for the outboard motor on our boat. It was certainly not enough for a dugout canoe and motor. And we would still have to return from Pelgrim Kondre to Moengo, by boat and then to Paramaribo by bus.

When we first arrived in Paramaribo it was the end of January 1964. Our superintendent had informed us immediately that the U.S. headquarters of the mission had not sent any money for us yet, but he would be able to advance money until our support arrived. Since we were living in a small home right next to the girls' school, he sent one of the girls over every day to go to the open market with Trudy, to buy food for us. Girls from the school even came to teach

Trudy how to prepare Suriname meals. The house, like many houses in the city, had no refrigerator. Therefore, food had to be bought every day. Trudy and I felt very bad that this man had to use his own money for us. That first month we bought the minimum of food. When we were asked if we needed stamps for our mail, or other items, we told him that we had some cash on hand. Everything else we wanted, in order to do housekeeping and other things, we did without. Certainly one day soon money would arrive. February being the shortest month of the year, our expenses were minimal.

Our superintendent informed us, at the end of that month, that our expenses for the month had been about fifty dollars. But since he expected our expenses to be higher in the town of Moengo, he was going to double that amount for every month. We would receive half of our support on the first of the month and the other half on the fifteenth.

One of the questions we had when we gave him our resignation was: How long would he continue to give us support? We had received the first part on the first day of the month. We resigned on the ninth day of the month and we never received any money from him again. Although we found out that two hundred dollars for that month were sent for us from the States, we had received only half of the promised monthly amount — half of what he had received for us.

Once we had taken care of the different matters in the city, we returned to Ricanau Moffo. Our first responsibility was to inform Captain Walter. Some of the villagers had mentioned to us on different occasions that they did not expect us to ever leave. "The house you have here is too nice to leave behind!" they said.

The evening of the day of our return to the village, we went over to see Captain Walter and shared with him our decision to leave his village. What a surprise to him! He had had no indication whatsoever that things had gone the way they did. Then he insisted on our telling him the reason for our leaving. We did not feel right about doing that. After all, we did not want to talk negatively about our superintendent, who was also the supervisor of the school for this village. But Walter insisted that we tell him. As Captain over his people, he needed to know. He then told us that we were not the first ones to leave the mission station and the work among his people. We told him again that he should receive that information from the pastor and not from us. He kept insisting, though, on hearing our side of the story first, and then later from this pastor. We felt compelled to tell him. We told him that we would be giving him our reasons for leaving, but that he would be hearing different reasons from pastor. Walter agreed to hear both reasons. After we had shared our side of the story, we also told him about what he probably would be hearing from the superintendent after we had left. Then he asked me if I could read a letter to him. It was a letter which he had already received from our superintendent (who wasn't our superintendent anymore). To our surprise and also to the Captain's surprise, the letter contained exactly what we had suspected would be given as the reason for our departure. Walter just wanted someone to read that letter to him, since he could not read himself. "This pastor will never come back to this village again!" Walter said, after having listened to the contents of the letter. That was his decision, and not ours!

The next two days were spent in packing our belongings and cleaning the house. Many different villagers came to say farewell. It was hard to leave these people, especially the six young men who had only a week or so before indicated to us their desire to follow Christ. How much we had longed to teach them more of the Word of God and to disciple them!

After we had loaded our things in the dugout canoe, we left for Moengo. Captain Walter was again willing to travel with us and bring back the boat, which did not belong to us anyway. We had purchased the motor. We were responsible for the monthly payments for the motor, as well as for the house. It did not seem right to leave the motor behind, for just anyone to use, and nobody to be responsible for it. Therefore we decided to take the motor back to the store where we had bought it. Our boat trip to Moengo took us much longer than usual. The big dugout canoe, with our belongings, was much slower than our speedboat. Once we had reached Moengo, Trudy and I decided that I would pick up our mail at the Post Office Box. We also had an almost empty gas cylinder for cooking. We could get back our deposit on it and thus have a few more dollars.

I first picked up the mail from the Post Office Box and took it back to the boat to give to Trudy. She was holding on to the high grass on the side of the river, while holding Rosyanne between her legs. After I handed her the mail, I took the gas cylinder back to the store, up a hill. It may have taken about thirty minutes before I returned to the river.

As I came down the hill again, to my surprise I saw Trudy in the boat out in the middle of the Cottica River. What in the world had happened? Trudy was not able to start the outboard motor again, so it took quite a while for her to get the boat back to shore, using her hands and flip flops. Then I found out why she had not held on to the grass. Among all the mail was a letter from her mother. Trudy had lost her dad during WW II. He had been taken away from the Netherlands by the Germans, although he was not in the age group of men who were taken to Germany to work during the first deportation. After he had fled from a camp, he had walked during the night hours and stayed in hiding during the day. Soon after he finally made it home, he was diagnosed with tuberculosis. Shortly after the war, he died.

While Trudy was still at home, her mother had received notification that she was eligible for financial compensation for what she had suffered during the war. But her mother did not feel right about claiming that money, as the Lord had supplied all her needs, both during the war and during all the years that followed. However, Trudy encouraged her mother to apply for the compensation anyway, since it was being distributed under a general German law covering all those who had suffered that kind of loss during the Nazi occupation of the Netherlands.

After all those many years, Trudy's mother had received her compensation and shared the news in that letter. She also wrote that she wanted to give us five hundred dollars for our ministry, and asked us to pray with her about what she could do with another five hundred dollars, also to be used in the Lord's work. One thousand dollars was the exact amount we would have to come up with to give to the government for our 'show-money', in order to stay in the country.

To our shame, we must admit that we never prayed, as Trudy's mother had asked. As soon as we could, we wrote her about the situation we were in. But God had already been providing for us, long before the need arose and through someone who had no idea of our needs, and who did not know the situation we were in.

"Wait on the Lord..." Psalms 37:34

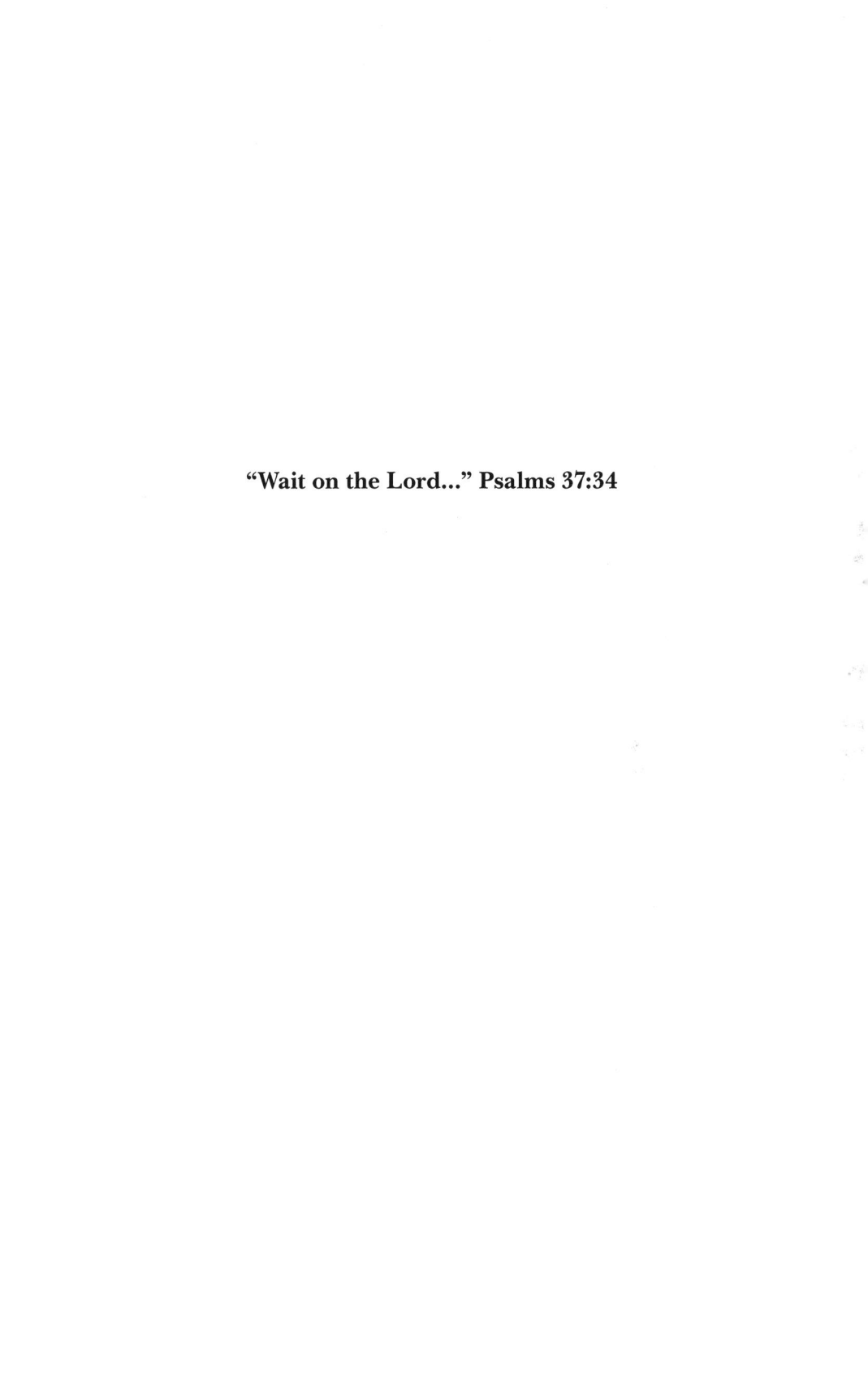

Chapter 7

Back in Paramaribo, November 1964

One of the first things we did in Paramaribo, after arriving there in November 1964, was to take the almost new outboard motor back to the storeowner. We explained the situation, and he was very willing to wait for us to tell him what we wanted to do next. The store owner, while in high school, had been a student of our superintendent.

Many more payments would still have to be made. From the storeowner we found out that our superintendent had cashed all the checks which we had sent, despite the fact that we had made out all checks to the store. Our superintendent, after cashing our checks, had each time made out a personal check to the storeowner. The contract had been between the store and us and only our name was on the papers.

It probably was the next day that we found out from the Bruynzeel Company that they had not received our checks either. We had faithfully sent in our monthly check to them, via our superintendent. Each check was made out to the company. The contract was between that company and us as well, but the company had received none of our payments. They had received personal checks from the pastor. We were advised to take both matters to court, but did not feel that it would be a good thing to do. After all, the Word of God does have something to say about taking fellow believers to court, in 1 Corinthians, Chapter 6.

We corresponded with family and friends in the days that followed. Another matter on our minds was the amount we owed to the government. What to do about the possibility of the Suriname officials asking us to leave the country? We went to the main police station and, asked to speak to the head of the office for foreigners. We explained very openly what our situation was and that we wanted to stay and be involved in some other missionary outreach. After hearing our story, this very kind officer told us that nobody could send us out of the country as long as we had not been involved in anything illegal.

He told us that we were there legally. When we asked him about the money that had been paid by an organization and that the same organization would be demanding the money back, he simply told us that there was no reason for the Suriname government to grant anyone that request.

At the same time he advised us to pay that amount as soon as possible, to get the other party off our backs. The fact that transferring the money from the Netherlands to Suriname would take some time was no problem in his eyes. It was another step in the right direction!

But our former superintendent was somehow able to get our address and he sent us a letter, which we received on December 5, 1964. The letter stated that return passage for us had been booked to return to Europe on a freighter. That was the way we had come to Suriname earlier that same year. He also informed us that if we did not accept his offer to return at that time, it would be our personal responsibility if we were to return later.

Early the next morning we headed for the offices of the Ship Company to inquire about the reservations that had been made for us. We found out that, just like the freighter that had brought us to Suriname, this ship had six cabins for twelve passengers. Trudy would be in one cabin with Rosyanne and another lady; I would be in a different cabin with another fellow. And we were informed that we had to confirm our departure with them that same day. We told them that we would let them know that day, but that we had no intention of leaving.

When we left the offices, I was feeling even worse physically than earlier that morning. We returned to our temporary home with our pilot friend and his family. As soon as we entered the house, Katie noticed that I wasn't looking so great and wondered what my problem was.

She immediately called her family physician, Dr. Jan van Mazijk. When he came over to the house to see me, he immediately made the diagnosis: "German measles! You are quarantined for 6 weeks," he said. Here was one more indication that we were not supposed to leave Suriname.

But now there was another complication: Trudy was pregnant with our second child, Artwin. She needed a shot to protect the baby from the harm German measles can cause an unborn baby. Dr. Jan soon found out that such shots were not available in the country. And we had heard already that such a shot would be very expensive, but God had made provisions for that need already. Why the Dutch military base in Suriname would have one shot available, I guess we will never know. And that they would make it available to us, at no cost at all, was only the Lord's doing. Trudy received that shot and within one week I was feeling well enough to start doing all kinds of things; even helping in the hangar in loading the mission plane and doing some purchasing for missionaries in the jungle.

Early during the month of December, Roy and Katie invited Dr. Jan and his wife Diet to come and spend an evening in their home. We learned much about the work among the Trio and Wayana Indians in the south of Suriname, just below the fourth parallel. That was the work Trudy and I had been interested in, while still in Europe. We had heard about that ministry while in France and later in England during linguistics training. We had even written to the leadership in Suriname, after getting the address from an anthropologist, who had spent some time with those tribes. However, we never received a reply.

That same week we contacted Dave Neff, the West Indies Mission field leader in Paramaribo, and when we asked about the letter we had sent in 1962, we found out that they had indeed received that letter, and still had it on file. The reason they had not answered us was the fact that two mission organizations were in the process of merging at that time. God has a reason for all these happenings and always He works out His perfect plan.

He was going to do that in the few weeks that were left of the year 1964!

Chapter 8

Missionary Team among Indians

During my years at the European Bible Institute near Paris in France, I had heard about a ministry among Indians in the south of Suriname. Again, while taking the linguistics course near London, England, we received more information from an anthropologist who had spent time among those tribes and liked what was going on among those people. However, contacting the leadership in Suriname was without result.

Now, while in Suriname, toward the end of 1964, we were able to meet the field leader in Suriname. At that time we were informed about the whole team:

Dave Neff, was the field leader, living in Paramaribo.

Don and Doris Draper lived in Paramaribo, and did the necessary shopping for the interior missionaries. They also took care of the daily radio communications. After the Drapers' return to the USA, Alice and Joel Nichols (Nick) took over that position.

There were two couples working among the Trios:
Claude and Barbara Leavitt were living in the village of Alalapadu;
Morgan and Mary Jane Jones were living in the village of Paloemeu.

There were also two couples working with the Wayana tribe:
Ivan and Doris Schoen lived in the village of Apetina, also called Big Arrow.
Walt and Marj Jackson lived in a village on the Lawa River, called Kawemhakan, or High Place.

These couples, except Dave Neff, started their ministry among the Indians under Door to Life Ministries, but later on organized as a Foundation, called Suriname Interior Fellowship, which eventually became part of West Indies Mission. Roy and Katie Parsons lived in the city of Paramaribo and Roy flew the mission plane and served under Mission Aviation Fellowship, often called MAF.

37

Wait on the Lord!" Psalm 37: 34

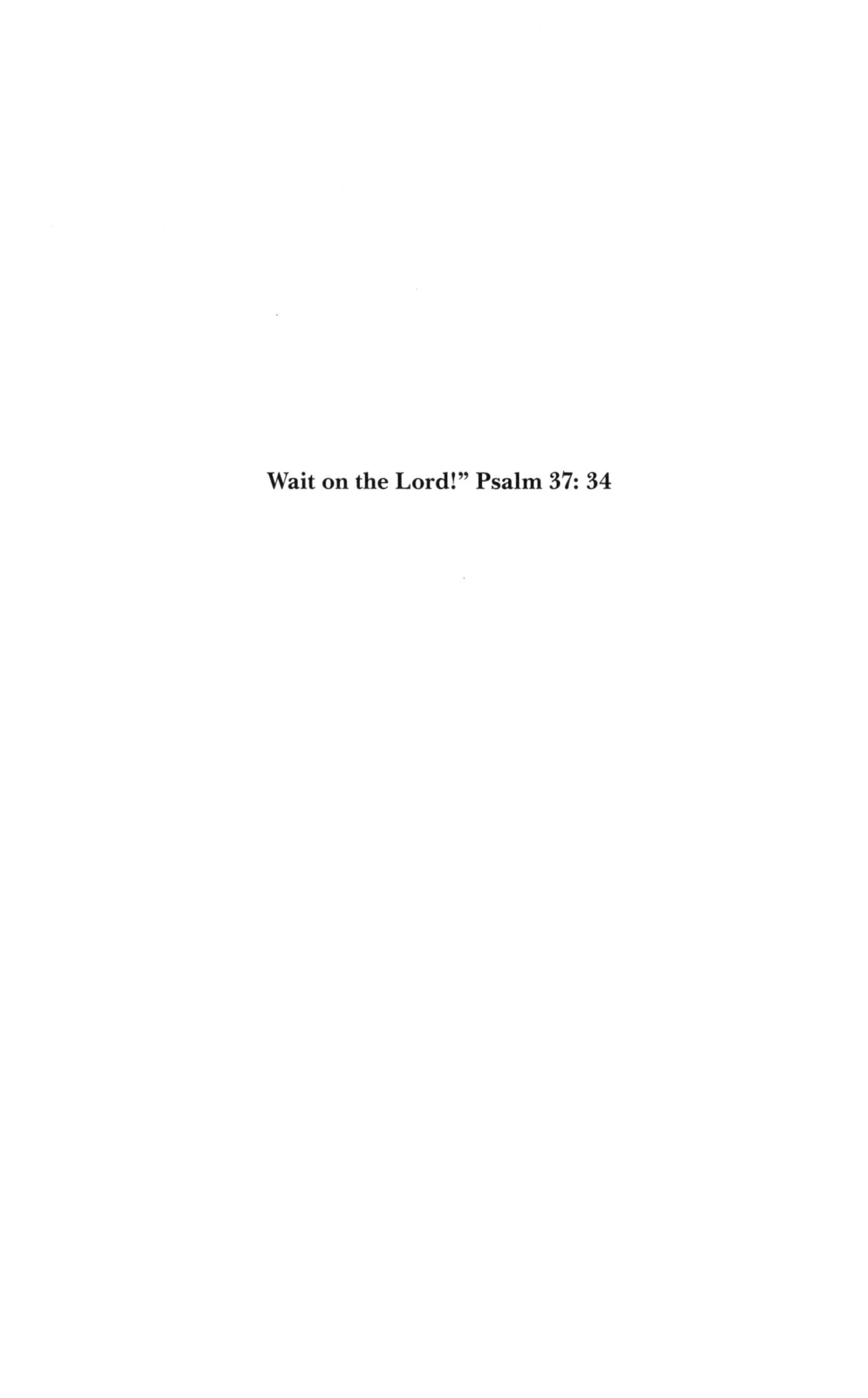

Chapter 9

Why Always that Waiting?

January 1965

Soon after our talk with Dr. Jan van Mazijk and his wife Diet, we visited their home and the church they attended. It was a mainly Dutch congregation, made up of all kinds of people with different church backgrounds. Dr. Jan, who was in charge of the medical work among the Indians, informed us of a very urgent need. Many Indians had been diagnosed with tuberculosis. The Suriname government, especially the Department of Health, was requesting that immediate attention be given to these people. Other Indian villages could be cared for by the missionaries present, but one village was vacant. Ivan and Doris Schoen had left the village of Big Arrow on the Tapanahony River, for a furlough in the United States.

Trudy, being an R.N., was the ideal person to do the medical work there. We had just applied to work under West Indies Mission and would need monthly support for a ministry among the Indians.

But what were the chances of raising support from a remote location like the village of Big Arrow? The monthly amount needed, which included personal support, flying, and station maintenance, was three hundred twenty-five dollars.

And where would we eventually be stationed? Walt and Marj Jackson were serving on the Lawa River among the Wayana Indians. Morgan and Mary Jane Jones were ministering among the Trio Indians at the mouth of the Paloemeu River, right where the Paloemeu River flows into the Tapanahony River. Both couples were leaving the field: one for a change of ministry and the other for time in the States. Both locations were presented to us as possibilities of ministry to the tribes which they were serving.

Nobody did any pushing at all in one direction or the other.

These missionaries firmly believed that the Lord of missions was going to direct our steps.

For us, it was a matter of finding the Lord's will.

When the request came from both the doctor and mission leadership to go to Big Arrow for several months, it meant that we did not have to decide right away which tribe we would be serving in the future. However, how were we going to find the support to go to this Wayana village and stay there for three or four months? How would we buy the supplies needed for all that time? At that time the MAF pilot, Roy, was grounded for medical reasons, and therefore the MAF plane could not take us to our destination. That would have been a flight of about seventy-five minutes.

Field leader Dave Neff told us to go ahead and buy the supplies we would need for the months to come. Money was made available to cover the cost. An empty government flight would take us, free of charge, to the airstrip of Paloemeu. From there Morgan Jones and a group of Trio Indians were going to take us downriver to the village of Big Arrow, which was also called by the name of the Indian chief Apetina, just downriver from the rock called Teboe. That name came from the Indian word tëpu, which means rock. It ended up becoming the name of that rock.

A not-very-young Beechcraft took us from Zorg and Hoop airport in Paramaribo to the beautiful grass jungle strip of Paloemeu. Morgan and his wife Mary Jane welcomed the three of us (we had Rosyanne, our 15-month-old daughter with us). The next morning Indian hammocks and food and our belongings were put in a dugout canoe, including the little bed we had brought for our daughter. Soon we started our trip down the Tapanahony River. We had no idea what to expect on this trip. Within a short time we found ourselves in the white water and rapids. Having known only the Cottica River, where large bauxite ships can travel, we were amazed when we saw how these Indians maneuvered the big dugout through the white water and in between the rocks — at times full speed ahead, when the waves were high, and at times slowly to keep the canoe from picking up water from the waves.

When we saw the first waterfalls we had no idea how we were going to get past them. But our Indian guides did know what to do.

First of all, they showed us what we were supposed to do — walk over certain rocks, or walk through the jungle. Always one of them would accompany us, because they felt a great responsibility to get us safely to our destination. They knew that the whole tribe would hold them accountable if something happened to us. We did not find this out until later.

At certain waterfalls the Indians could take the whole canoe with all the contents through some channel of water. Sometimes they would completely empty the canoe and carry all the cargo to the other side of the falls and manage the canoe through some wild water. We learned these things, in order to do them ourselves later! At times that meant going over steep places, but there were also times that the whole canoe had to be dragged over the rocks and sometimes even through the jungle. Going downriver and down the rocks and hills in the jungle was one thing, but of course people had to return the same way. Later on, we made that same trip up and down that river several times, and we had those experiences many times.

By four in the afternoon it was time to stop and find a place to spend the night. We had brought two hammocks with pretty thick cotton mosquito nets; one for Trudy and Rosyanne and one for me. Simple huts were fixed up which offered us shelter in case of rain. The hammocks were quickly tied underneath the thatch roofs. We ate our evening meal with our Indian friends: the fish that some of them had caught, along with cassava bread and fish broth with plenty of salt and pepper. By six thirty in the afternoon, or should we say evening, it was dark. Trudy and I therefore rapidly disappeared into our hammocks and so did our senior missionary Morgan.

The Indians carried on for a long time. It seemed like all night. When we woke up some time during the night we heard a terrible noise in the jungle, but had no idea what it could be. It sounded like a big monster somewhere close by. Trudy eventually called out to me to ask what I thought it could be. The only answer I could come up with, to give both her and myself peace of mind, was to say that the Indians did not seem to be alarmed and therefore we should not be either. At times we heard the Trios laugh or someone rapidly walk by our hut. Then we could hear some water splash or a stick hitting the rocks. We had no idea what was going on.

When it became light again, we asked Morgan about the different noises we had heard and what the Indians had been doing during the night. We found out that some had been fishing. Others had been having fun with an alligator, which had been hiding in a puddle in the rocks, close to our hut. They do eat alligators and we do too, but the water of the puddle was not clean enough and therefore they had not wanted to kill and eat it. The terrible noise we had heard had come from a group of howler monkeys somewhere in the jungle — a noise which we have heard many times since. It had echoed to the other side of the wide river.

After our breakfast with the Indians, we continued our journey on the river. Just a couple more waterfalls, but those were not the most impressive. Or maybe we were getting used to them already. At one of them we met a group of Wayana Indians, who were on their way to Paloemeu. Immediately we were invited to have breakfast with them as well. Right away we noticed that they used a lot more pepper in their broth than Trios do, something we would get used to in the months to come.

By noon we reached the village of Big Arrow and were led to a house which belonged to the Schoen family. Everything had to be brought out of storage: beds, chairs, linens and kitchen utensils. There was firewood underneath the jungle house and we needed to start a fire in the wood stove, to make something to eat for lunch. Then it was time to put up the antenna and try out our two-way radio. That would keep us in touch with Paramaribo. We could not expect the plane to come in during our stay in the village. Everything found a place in the house and everything worked. Although we had kerosene lamps, we still decided to go to sleep early. Almost two days on the river and in the wind and sunshine had tired us out, especially because of all the new impressions.

We had a good night's rest.

Getting the wood stove fired up again in the morning was not all that simple. The firewood was damp. Just the thought that we had to go through this ritual, day after day, was daunting! We needed warm water for our coffee and for Rosyanne's food. Soon after breakfast Morgan announced that he did not see the need to stay another day, but asked us at the same time what we thought about it. We had spent six months alone at Ricanau Moffo and did not see the need either for him to stay longer. We would do okay. And we did very well that first week. Don Draper, a missionary in the city was, by radio, in contact with all the missionaries. He was also in charge of all purchasing for the interior workers. Fortunately, we didn't need anything; even if we had needed something, there would have been no way to get it to us. The plane would not fly for quite a long time.

The following week, during one of the radio contacts, we discovered that our transmitter did not work anymore. We could hear the other missionaries talk and we heard Paramaribo call the village of Apetina, or Big Arrow. But they could not hear us. There was never any concern on our part, but in the city people began to worry after several days. Each time they called us, we would try to answer, but there was no transmission. Finally, one of the missionaries, on another station, mentioned that he thought that he could hear the click of our mike. We were asked if we were still standing by and if we were able to hear them. We answered by clicking the button on our mike. Sure enough, they could hear it.

In order to make sure that they indeed heard what they thought they heard, we were asked to click the mike twice. It worked! No transmission, but just those clicks, and now we were able to 'communicate' again. We were asked certain questions and we could answer them with either one or two clicks. All of us felt good about this. We could at least let them know whether things were okay with us or not.

Trudy became very involved with the people through her medical work, while I spent a great deal of time with the men of the village. They wanted me to hunt and fish with them as well. I could communicate with most of them in the language we had learned in Ricanau Moffo: Sranang Tongo.

Nuwahe, the chief on that river, came over to our hut on Saturday and wanted to know if I would like to go hunting with him and some others. "Sure, but I have no shotgun!" I said. No problem. He provided one, plus the shells. Off we went, through the waterfalls and to the other side of the river, into the jungle. A new experience! Up one hill, and down on the other side; wade through a creek, up another hill and down again. And, sure enough, there was our first prey — a wild pig, called pakira, or pecari in English, the kind with a white ring around the neck. The wild pigs travel through the jungle as a couple or as a family. Nuwahe cleaned out the inside and left it there. Maybe an hour later, after more up and down different hills and through swamps, we saw a deer. Now it was my turn to shoot. Great! I got it right the first time. Same procedure as with the pig. Then he quickly cut into a tree, to get a long piece of bark. He tied it around the deer and then lifted it up to put it on my shoulders and back. For them it is: What you kill, you carry home. Thanks! The animal was still dripping blood a little bit, and carried ticks. We had to go back to the village. Same way: up and down, through creeks and swamps again. It was a good thing that Nuwahe knew where we were going. I would have gone the opposite direction. After coming back to the spot where he shot the pig, he did the same thing: a strip of bark, and up on his shoulders and back.

Eventually I could hear the waterfalls by the village. That was my Saturday, ending with a terrible headache, and feeling extremely tired.

I sure slept that night!

On Sunday we joined the village residents for the service in their big round hut, which was the church. That afternoon all the Indians went to a sandbar in the river. The men wrestled each other and the women just moved their hands in the water, making a terrific noise. I was challenged to wrestle some of the men. And you know what? I threw them in the river, as I had more strength for a minute or so. However, if I could not throw one in the water right away, I was the conquered one.

Hunting on Saturdays was not my thing. I was asked the following week to join Nuwahe again. That was the last time I agreed to go on such a grueling trip. When Nuwahe asked me again, I simply told him that I did not want to go.

The following week on a different day he had a different invitation: going out at night to hunt for alligators and a certain kind of rodent. That was a wonderful experience. Shooting alligators in the dark, as they were sitting on rocks or on the riverbank, meant that everything you shot was simply put in the canoe. On the way back to the village Nuwahe caught several dozen catfish that were just floating in the water, on shallow rocks. He used his machete to cut them up. Good meat!! How I enjoyed spending those hours with Nuwahe!

Whether I was there in the jungle or on the river, the thought always came to me: "What a rich reality: God sees us here! We are far away from villages and people, and what is called civilization and all the noise and busyness, but God is here."

All three of us – Trudy, Rosyanne, and I — enjoyed the daily times by the river and in the water. We washed ourselves in the river, as well as our clothes and dishes, and played with a number of the Wayana children in the water. It may have been their assignment by their parents to keep an eye on us when we went to the river, because they seemed to always follow us when we moved in the direction of the Tapanahony River. Some of these same children would swim a little upstream from the rapids near the village and then drift with the water to the next bunch of rocks on the other side of the rapids. Then they would follow the same procedure and go to the next rock formation. It looked as though it was dangerous, when we watched them the first time, but it didn't take too long for us to start doing it with them. Quite adventurous for both of us, but especially for Trudy who was in the fifth month of her second pregnancy! I started out going by myself, following the Indian children. Then Trudy tried it and I had Rosyanne on my back; she was really hanging on tightly.

Going . . . ! A Sacrifice?

After three months in the village of Big Arrow, the missionary pilot from the neighboring country, then called British Guyana, came over to Suriname to do some much-needed flying. Dr. Jan took advantage of his presence by planning a medical trip to some of the Indian villages, including Apetina, Big Arrow. It was so good to have that kind of contact with the outside world. Trudy wanted the doctor to see a number of the people, including a lady who had some kind of tumor. It was decided to remove the growth, there and then, in our extra bedroom. Not knowing what kind of growth it was and not wanting to take any risk, it was decided that Dr. Jan would take the removed growth with him to the city in order to have it checked in the lab. The surgery had gone very well and both Trudy and Jan were relieved. This was the last patient they checked and so all instruments were picked up and put away. Only the tumor needed to be put in something. But when the right container was found for it, the tumor could not be found anymore. We looked under the stretcher and on the floor, on and under the chair and even under the house. The floor had cracks in it, as it had been made of slats made from the bark of a palm tree. Those cracks would have been too small for the tumor to fall through anyway. The only solution we could come up with was that the cat had silently come in and stolen 'his lunch'! There apparently was no problem after removing that growth, because the Indian lady remained in good health after the operation.

Before the plane came back to pick up the doctor, we talked about Trudy's pregnancy and it seemed better to all three of us for her to go back to the city as soon as an opportunity arose. That opportunity arrived later. Trudy went to Paramaribo for her last weeks of pregnancy and I followed later. But first of all I spent some time at Paloemeu. During the months at Apetina the Lord had directed our thoughts more and more toward the Trio Indians in that village at the mouth of the Paloemeu River.

There was still a house available on that station, where the first missionary pilot Ted Lepper and his wife Nancy had lived. Nancy was the medical doctor who had come to Suriname with the original missionaries who started the work among the Trio and Wayana Indians. Their mission was called Door to Life and had become part of West Indies Mission at the time that we contacted them in the early sixties. During the interim period, the missionaries had organized as Suriname Interior Fellowship, at the recommendation of officials in Paramaribo. All missionary work south of the fourth parallel was given to S.I.F.

Our house in Ricanau Moffo had a metal roof. The Schoens' house at Apetina had a thatch roof. Our senior missionaries wondered how we were going to put a wood stove in a house with a thatch roof. Even the Schoens had a metal roof on the part of the house where their wood stove was located. We made it known that we were not going to have a wood stove, but a gas stove — the one we had already used in Ricanau Moffo, which had been given to us before we went to Suriname.

At first, this idea did not sit well with our colleagues in Paloemeu. After all, the Indian women needed to be able to earn some money and the only way they could do that would be to provide our firewood. At that time, we were more interested in Trudy's convenience. Getting up in the middle of the night to start a wood fire and warm a bottle for a baby had not been a very positive experience. We were also expecting Artwin. You needed about one quart of kerosene to start a fire with the wet firewood. Plus there would be other activities and jobs for the women. They could clean around their own huts and therefore could clean around our big hut too. They were anxious to keep the whole mission station clean as well.

Less than one year later most of the other missionaries were also using gas burners and stoves. It made the lives of the women so much easier and gave them more time to spend talking with the people and learning their language.

Upon arrival in Paramaribo, we got some very good news about our needed monthly support. Dr. Jan's sister-in-law had been busy. When she had heard that we needed to have three hundred twenty-five dollars support per month, for working among Indians in the interior of Suriname, she wondered why we would have to find that support ourselves. It would be much better if, after leaving the village of Big Arrow and the Wayana Indians, we would be able to go straight to the place where God wanted to place us. She and some others in the church in the city began to share the need for our support. Now the total amount had been pledged, mostly by career people from the Netherlands, and three couples from the US, working for Alcoa. God had provided, just as He had done so often before and would do again in the more than fifty years to come.

"Things heard…things taught…things transferred…!"
2 Timothy 2:2

Chapter 10

Starting Life among the Trios

Trudy and I officially began our time among the Trios at Paloemeu during the last days of June 1965, less than two weeks after Artwin was born.

On one of the first evenings after our arrival, we met with the Indian church leaders, who had just been appointed by Morgan Jones and the believers. Morgan had decided that it was the best way to leave the small group of believers, as nobody knew whether or not there would be someone to carry on the work among them after his departure. The meeting took place in our house, in what we used to call the 'Indian room'. Actually it was the first room one entered as soon as one climbed the stairs of our house, which was built about seven feet off the ground. This is where the Indians could sit or stand and watch us in our living room, kitchen, and office space. No privacy!

Morgan informed me that I had to prepare a Bible lesson for these men, which I was supposed to teach in less than six weeks, because we would be on our own after that time. This meant that all my time would have to be spent in language study. It was! Six days per week and a minimum of eight hours a day. There really was no choice. It was going to be a matter of 'jumping in the water' and 'swim or sink'.

The first lesson dealt with the fig tree in Luke 13:6-9. I must have actually translated those verses myself with the help of a Trio and my senior missionary, Morgan. In the Trio language the verbs are the most important and it was easy to remember the nouns. I wrote out the whole lesson and then more or less memorized it. The evening I presented the teaching to those men, I only had some verbs and conjugations on a piece of paper. This lesson is something I have never forgotten and to our astonishment we found out, many years later, that some of those men had not forgotten it either. The main lesson of bearing fruit, for the Indians, is something we have seen over these many years. But we will come to that subject later.

Language study continued. We did this in a number of ways. At times I would just take part of the Gospel of Mark, which Morgan had translated already. Then I would mark those words, or parts of words, which I knew already. With the limited grammar booklet, I would then look up those things I did not know. During the first six weeks I could still go over to Morgan's place, on the other side of the mission station and closer to the main part of the village.

He could answer all our questions. We marveled at the great knowledge he had of the Trio language, but of course he had taken the same linguistics course that I had. He also gave me his file of verbs to copy, probably close to eight hundred. Each verb could be changed by adding 'suffixes'. That way we had about five thousand verbs.

At other times I would take my tape recorder and sit down with some Indians. I would either record what they were saying as they were talking to one another, or I would ask them questions and they would answer me. Then I would take the recording home and listen to it. Subsequently I would rewind it, and listen to what I thought was one sentence, and write it down. Of course there was quite a bit of rewinding since I couldn't catch all the words the first time.

Eventually everything was on paper and I would try to dissect the language, as I did with passages in the Gospel of Mark. Frequently I would go back to Morgan again and ask him about the things that puzzled me.

After six weeks, when our senior missionary left, we continued the same activities, plus some other things. For instance, we would tape a service in the church building, except for the singing. All the services were conducted by the Indians. There were about seventy believers at that time. First, one would get up and lead in the singing, from the small song books which had been made for them by Morgan. Another person would get up and lead the others in quoting Bible verses, which they had learned by heart. Others could read them as well from a little booklet which many of them possessed.

A third person would lead in prayer and the next one would read from the Gospel of Mark. All the church leaders had learned to read and write. We call them elders in this book, but in the Trio language they are called 'educators'; maybe the better translation would be 'up-bringers'. Then the teacher would follow. He would read a verse and share his thoughts, then read another verse and give some more information, from time to time making some personal applications. As they did not have other Bible books in their language, it was not possible to go to other books or verses. Once I was home again, I would follow the same steps again: write down what I had on the tape and translate it the best I could.

I found that another good way to learn their language was to have an Indian conjugate a verb while I put it on a tape. Actually he would say it twice on the tape, like: I hunt…I hunt. Then: you hunt…you hunt.

I made longer or shorter loops of the reel-to-reel tape and let them run through my recorder and over some nails, which I had put in the rafters of our thatched roof. All kinds of different lengths were made as we had put many nails in the rafters. We also had tapes with verbs, or greetings, or short sentences. Not only did that help me to learn the language, but it also helped Trudy. We would listen to those tapes even while doing other things. Sometimes Trudy would be preparing our meals or sewing, and at times both of us were taking care of our mail.

We found out, however, that the Trios were very polite. They would hardly ever correct our mistakes. Sometimes we would catch ourselves or each other making a mistake. When we asked the Indians why they did not correct us, they said: "We understood what you said!" For weeks I had been making the same grammatical error. Each evening I would go over to one corner of the mission station, where our gas generator was located. When the people who lived closest to our house asked me what I was going to do, I always gave them the same response. Of course they knew exactly what I was going to do, but they would ask anyway. In English I would have said: "I am going to start the generator." But in Trio I was supposed to say the equivalent of:

"I go starting the generator." While going through one of my recordings, I noticed how they said things, like my daily answer about starting the generator. I quickly went to see one of my language helpers and asked him about this matter. He told me that what I had on the tape was the correct way of saying it. I asked: "So what I say to you every night about the generator is not correct?" He then proceeded to tell me that indeed that was not correct in the Trio language. I then asked him why nobody had ever corrected me over all that time. He replied:

"We all understood what you meant!"

Let me assure you that this made me a little unhappy with them! I made it very clear to them that we wanted to be corrected when we made a mistake in speaking their language. "That will be the only way for us to learn your language correctly!" I said. From that time on, they did occasionally correct us, and some still do from time to time.

By August 1965 we had had several meetings with the leaders in our house. They discussed certain situations in the church and the people in the village. Each meeting started with a time in the Word, and I had to prepare that lesson. Then several led in prayer. At that time they presented the matters they wanted to discuss - something like an agenda for the evening. Trudy always had tea with lots of sugar for them. This was a real treat and they expressed their appreciation to their 'mother' or 'older sister'. Only one of them called her 'my daughter'. That was Korokoro, who later moved back to Brazil, where he had come from. He passed away in 2000, just months after one of the Indians had taken his picture, with an instamatic camera we gave them.

During those meetings, the leaders would immediately ask me how to handle the particular situation or person under discussion. My reply was always: "How would you do that?" They would then discuss it for quite a while and come up with some solution from what they had of God's Word. At times I told them something from the Bible: a story or a verse. These things helped me decide what other portion or stories from the Bible I would translate next. James, being a very practical book, was one of the first ones they received from me. This was the way all these evenings were spent. Sometimes these meetings lasted until deep into the night. Of course, we could have given them the answers to all their questions and gone to bed early, but our goal was to train leaders who eventually would lead the congregation on their own.

2 Timothy 2:2 was taught over and over again during the years at EBI in France. This was the teaching we wanted to put into practice! "And the things that thou hast heard from me, among many witnesses, the same commit thou to faithful men, who shall be able to teach others also!"

"...much people was added unto the Lord..." Acts 11: 24

Chapter 11

The Move to PËRËRU TËPU, 1966

During one of our weekly meetings, in our Indian room, Trudy and I were informed by the church leaders that quite a large group of the Indian population would be leaving a few days later, to go upriver and cut new gardens. During the six weeks when Morgan was still with us, he had told us about the possibility that the Paloemeu people might be leaving the village in order to start a new village. He had no idea where that village might be located.

Most of the people were fed up with the tourists who visited their village, especially on Sundays. When a DC 3 landed with twenty-two of them, half of them would hurry to the village, while the morning service still had not ended. Some of them would be looking into that big round thatched roof building and hanging over the enclosure, made of split palm bark. Other people would also visit at other times. Some of them treated the Indians harshly and talked loudly to them. Often a woman or girl was misused by workmen in the area. We were frequently informed by one Indian or another that a tourist had come into his hut and taken something from him — either a set of bow and arrows, or some beadwork or an Indian comb. They then proceeded to show us what they had received as payment: two dimes or a couple of cigarettes.

We were able to make some changes that helped the Indians. We offered to buy the Indian artifacts from them and pay them right away. When the tourists arrived, usually during the Sunday morning church service, they were informed that all Indian souvenirs could be purchased in our house. The chief pilot in those days, of Suriname Airways, was very happy about this arrangement. He had felt bad on many occasions when the people he had brought left with so many items, for which they had paid so little. During the week one or other of the men would come to our house, to check the length of his bow to know how much money he would be getting. Trudy was always very strict when she checked the quality of the artifacts. We both wanted to be sure that the tourists would receive authentic items of very good quality and not something just made for tourists. Now the tourists received authentic Trio curios of high quality.

This arrangement made us happy too, because both the Indians and the tourists were satisfied. We made it clear, however, to the Indians, that we were selling their artifacts for a little higher price than they had received for them. We used the profit to pay for everything that was used for their literacy program, including the newly translated Bible portions. The Indians were very happy about this arrangement. They received more for their artifacts than ever before. Every so often we conducted school for those who wanted to learn to read. We had mimeographed eight booklets. Most of them learned to read their own language in about six weeks.

But even the arrangements we made about tourism did not change the minds of the village residents. They still wanted to have their own village. According to the philosophy of these Indians, they did not own the land they were living on. They had the tradition that the person who started cutting some place in the jungle, or gave the order to cut it, was automatically the owner of that piece of land. Those who came to live there, did accept the fact that this particular Indian was the owner and had all the authority and respect accorded to that position.

The problem with the village at the mouth of the Paloemeu was that people from the north, 'pananakiris', had started cutting that area. The government of Suriname had cleared an area to build an airstrip. All of this was part of Operation Grasshopper. Many of those strips had been built in the interior of Suriname. Apparently the Indians had chosen the new location already, but none of the missionaries were included in their planning. No reason for including us, anyway. We were their guests!

The following Monday we watched many Indians leave in their canoes, up the Tapanahony River. They were headed for Toad Rock, which was called Përeru Tëpu in Trio, and they stayed there close to two months.

When we, with our children Rosyanne and Artwin, left for Paramaribo to do some necessary shopping, we were flown over the newly cut area, southwest of Paloemeu. It was quite a sight, this large half circle, which the Indians had cut in the jungle.

Soon after we returned to Paloemeu, the Indians returned as well. All the trees which had been cut needed to dry for a period of time. Several months later the Indians returned to their cutting and started burning and cleaning the area. Only some temporary huts had been built near the riverside. The whole area was going to be gardens, where cassava or manioc, bananas and sweet potatoes would be planted. It was a combined effort by all the Paloemeu Indians. Many trips were made to transport the planting materials from their gardens at Paloemeu, to this location about forty miles upstream. Once that was done, everybody returned to Paloemeu and hardly any mention of the new village was made in the months that followed.

But sometime during the month of August in 1966, the news came to us from the same men. They were leaving the village of Paloemeu and moving to Toad Rock. Now we needed to make some decisions.

We had talked to our mission leader in the city and other colleagues. We discussed the situation also with Dr. Jan, who was not only involved in the medical work in our village, but in three other locations. The government was very much interested in making sure that the Indians were well taken care of.

From time to time, when we were in the city, some worker from a company involved in making an inventory of the different minerals in Suriname, would send an urgent and panic-producing radio message to the city. The doctor was informed that either some Indians were very sick or someone was dying. Those messages usually resulted in a plane being sent in to check out the situation.

Often, the so-called dying person was either up and around or out fishing or hunting. The 'very sick' people either had a headache or a cold. After consulting with the different people involved, in the city, it was decided that we would stay at Paloemeu if fifteen or more Indians continued to live there.

That would mean that the ones at Përéru Tëpu would be without medical care.

In discussing the matter with the leaders, we were told that only two individuals and their families would be staying behind. The men were employed by those who were in charge of the airstrip. The total number of Indians staying at Paloemeu would be less than fifteen. It was in August 1966 that our family made the first visit to the new location. It was a tremendous joy for us to meet such a happy Indian community. Finally, they had their own land again! Nobody would just come in and do what visitors used to do in Paloemeu.

But now we had to get involved ourselves. The Indians wanted to build an airstrip. If someone were seriously ill, they would have to be flown to the hospital in Paramaribo. They wanted all supplies for school and church and our family to be flown in directly to the new village. All the other main villages of

Trio and Wayana Indians had an airstrip, so they wanted one too. And they were willing to do all the work, if we could provide the equipment: shovels, rakes, axes and files, etc. The Indians also wanted to know where to build the runway and how long and how wide it had to be. We could only imagine to a certain degree how much work was awaiting us. The people themselves needed better huts, because in just a few months the rains would be coming. They needed to cut more jungle for gardens. We were offered a nice hut of nine by twelve feet, just by the rock at the entrance of the village. The hut was divided by us, into two parts. The smaller part was our bedroom, for the four of us. The larger part was our living room, kitchen, office and clinic, all at the same time. After seven months, when we had our own house, this hut became a temporary clinic.

Roy, our mission pilot, and his wife Katie made the next trip from Paloemeu to Tepoe with us. He helped with the lay-out and direction of the runway. Soon the work on this new airstrip started. It was going to be right through the gardens which the Indians had cut and planted the previous year. They needed the food anyway, but the food was being used much faster than we had hoped.

One year is really not long enough to get the kind of manioc tubers that will be big enough to feed that many people. However, they still had their gardens at Paloemeu.

Now the commuting began. Several families returned to the village in Paloemeu, which they had left, to make enough cassava bread for one month. The following week more families left to do the same thing. After three weeks or more the first families returned and they all took turns making the trip downstream to get more food. The progress in building the airstrip was slow.

When friends in Paramaribo began asking questions about our progress and the food situation, one of them came up with a great suggestion. This man was in charge of the food supply for the Dutch army in the country. From time to time old supplies were done away with and new supplies were brought in. "Could we use any of the old supplies?" we were asked. The list included rice and oil and raisin bread in cans, sugar and salt, and many more things like that. We sure could, but would we be able to get everything to Toad Rock? "Well," said our friend, "if somebody were to offer me an elephant, I would not accept it either. I would not know how to feed one! But you think about it and let me know."

When some business people, whom we knew from the church in Paramaribo, heard about this possibility, they offered help. I then had the opportunity to speak to many more business men who belonged to the Rotary Club in Paramaribo. "Religion and politics are never brought up in our meetings, but you may freely speak about your missionary work, without asking for money!" I was told. So I did and told them the whole story, including what God had done and was doing for the Indians. Together these men were willing to pay for all the necessary flights from Paramaribo to Paloemeu, plus all the transportation to Tepoe by canoes. Our friend from the military promised to provide at least one ton, and possibly two tons, of food. It would be delivered to the Mission Aviation Fellowship hangar. We returned to Toad Rock, Përëru Tëpu, or as it eventually became known by the outside world, Tepoe.

The next day, during the early radio contact to give our weather report, we received a message from Roy about the food supply. We were told that the army trucks had just arrived and that there was a pile of six tons of food, ready to be flown to Paloemeu, and that the first donation had already come in, to pay for transportation.

I met the first plane load with food that came in to Paloemeu. Some of this food was tried out, already, by those in the canoes during the trip to Tepoe. From that time on, many boat trips were made and much progress in building the strip was made. The people at Tepoe had probably never worked that hard before, and at the same time they had never looked as healthy, either. Most of them put on weight!

One week before Christmas, Roy came back to Tepoe by canoe, with the last load of food and other supplies. He checked out the strip. We had a little more than one thousand feet cleared and ready. The only problem was that the surface was too soft. "If you can do anything to make the surface harder, I will try to make my first landing on December 26th!" he said. Then he left for Paloemeu again by canoe.

Because of all the river trips, which had been made to get all the supplies from Paloemeu to Tepoe, we had many empty fifty-five gallon drums. We had started organizing game days the year before. This was done to fill a void in the lives of the Indians, after they had stopped their wild parties with much drinking and dancing. We decided to fill those empty drums with water and sand from the river. On our game day we introduced a new game: four or five Indians rolling just as many drums down the runway for about fifty feet. Then the next group would compete, followed by the next volunteers. We had not yet seen these people have so much fun! But what they did not know at that time was the reason for having those races. After the plane landed on December 26th, the pilot told them that they had done a wonderful job in hardening the surface of the runway! We celebrated the occasion! Then we told the Indians why they had been rolling those heavy drums!

With this job behind us, the Indians began to concentrate on planting their new gardens. It was the right time, because the short rainy season had started but, at the same time, they were talking about our housing situation. They must have discussed the matter with each other prior to the time when one of the leaders came over to our hut to tell us that they wanted to build our house. That was something they had promised us to do, even before we left our remodeled house in Paloemeu. The verbal agreement, which they had agreed on among themselves, was that the house would be built at no cost to us. But here they were. Many did not have their own permanent huts yet. When we objected to our house being built at that time, they said: "You are not Indians and should not be living on a dirt floor!"

At that point we suggested to them that they appoint a certain number of men to help us build our house. All of them would start collecting the materials from the jungle, especially the leaves for the roof. Then some of the group would start helping us to put up the frame of the house. All of the workers would at the end receive the same amount of money. It helped us and them at the same time.

Our house was built in a short time and we moved into it. The hut we had been living in was turned into a temporary clinic.

There was a wonderful atmosphere in the village and the church began to thrive. Month after month we heard confessions of faith. The elders were doing a great job in leading the church members, and they received respect and support from the people.

Our time for our first furlough drew nearer. At the same time, efforts were made to reach Indians from another tribe in French Guyana. Some of us missionaries and the field leader for Suriname, Dave Neff, went to St. Laurent in French Guyana, to present a plan to start working among an Indian tribe there. The request was turned down, as the officials were convinced that we missionaries had nothing to offer to these people that they could not offer to them. Offering the glorious Gospel of our Lord Jesus Christ to them was not something they wanted to consider.

This did not stop the Tepoe church from sending one missionary team to those Indians. They were flown from Tepoe to the Wayana village on the Lawa river. It was a nonproductive trip, as many villages did not even want to receive these Indian missionaries.

In the other villages there was no real interest either.

However, God did have a plan for these Medeyo Indians!

Just after our Indian missionaries had flown from Tepoe to begin their missionary trip, we left Tepoe, to begin our first furlough in Europe. Just before we left, we had received the news that the new pilot in charge of the missionary flying program had closed our airstrip and demanded that a new strip be built. His decision was based on a diagram, which some college students had made, of the strip and the terrain beyond it. Unfortunately two different scales had been used: one for the whole length of the runway plus the fly-out area, and one for the difference in altitude of the surface of the strip. The way it was drawn up, it looked like the village and the strip were located in a big hole and the area beyond the runway was made up only of high mountains!

And they spoke the Word of God with boldness! Acts 4:31

CHAPTER 12

What We Learned from the Trios

It was always such a joy to teach the Trio people and to experience how they taught others — not only those of their own tribe, or of other tribes in Suriname, but also people from tribes across the borders. We will not forget the lessons we ourselves learned from them.

We think of the time, for instance, when we were spending some days with a group of Indians near, and in, one of the waterfalls. As I struggled through the whitewater in that rivers, I followed one of the men, while another Trio followed me. We had to be careful about where to put our feet. Sometimes there were shallow places and at times deeper spots. If a spot was too deep, there was the danger of just being swept away by the swift running water. Or you could bump your toes or your knees on some rock.

When I noticed a rock very close to me, I tried to go around it and warned Atinijo, who was right behind me. "Be careful, there is a rock here!" I said to him. He answered: "That rock is there for us to step on!" Quite a different way of thinking! What a lesson I learned from this young Indian. I had seen that particular rock as an obstacle and danger, whereas he saw it as a stepping stone to go where he wanted to go. When God places obstacles in our way, it is not to make us stumble, but to help us reach our goal!

Then we also think about the times when we found ourselves in a difficult situation on the river or during other activities with our Indian friends. So often our mode of operation is to talk about the situation and try to find a solution for the problem we are facing. It felt almost as though we were being appropriately reprimanded by these people, when they said: "Our God is going to help us to get through this situation again!" Or: "Let us talk to our Father first!"

On trips through the jungle, in places where the Indians had never been, they too did wonder at times which direction to go — maybe on this side of a mountain or maybe on the other side. Or they wondered whether or not they should cross a creek. Even in those circumstances they would first turn to Him, Who Knows the Way. When a river is high, due to heavy rains, it is not always clear to them where they should take the canoe through the rapids. At those times, as well, they 'make their requests...known to God!'

What wonderful applications we have heard when Indian believers taught things about the Word which they had learned from us.

After I had translated the book of Jonah in the sixties, I taught it for quite a number of hours during the week. On one of the following Sundays, Naki, who was one of the church leaders, decided to bring a message on Jonah. After reading a portion of the book, and leading in prayer, he started out by asking a question: "What was Jonah's threefold sin?" It made me think. It was certainly not one of the lessons I had taught, but then he gave the three-point outline of his message.

Three points! Again something he had not been taught yet. First of all, he pointed out that God told him to go and Jonah said: "NO!" And he fled from the face of the Lord. Secondly, he told everyone that Jonah should have prayed, but instead he slept. While the pagan sailors all turned to their gods, God's servant had 'turned in'. And thirdly, Naki pointed out that Jonah did not use the means that God had given him to make God's name great. He paid the owner of the ship, in order to flee from the presence of the Lord. Jonah could have spent his money on many other things, which would not have been against God's will. But Jonah engaged in actions that were indeed against God's revealed will.

How many times have we heard Trio Indians say that it was good for them to go and tell others about the One they 'are onto'? With that they mean the One they believe in, or trust. "We too were ignorant about Him, and our teachers came to tell us. Now we know the One we are onto!" they said. "But our family members, members of other tribes, do not know Him. Let us go and make this Good News to be heard by them! The thing that is a-glad-making-one, we must tell!"

O yes! They have been taught, but have developed by themselves wonderful ways to make the teaching of God's Paper clear to their hearers, in their own and related cultures.

Going . . . ! A Sacrifice?

We were struck when we heard one of the Indians teach on the filling of the Spirit. I had used illustrations from our culture, even an object lesson. After sharing some of the Bible passages with all of us, he came up with an illustration from his own culture. He talked about the big gourds they used in those days. Almost every family had one or more, just outside their hut. It was always kept on the shady side of the hut. He said: "All of us individually are like one of those gourds. We know what happens to a full gourd, outside our hut, when the wind blows. That gourd is going to stay right there. The wind is not able to pick it up, or turn it over. That is because there is water in it. And when it is empty, you women go back to the river and fill it up again. That is how it works, when we are filled with the Spirit of God. The devil cannot move us. We stay there where God has placed us and we are useful. But when that gourd is empty and you do not take the time to go to the river to fill it up again, something else will happen when the wind blows. The wind will blow it over and roll it in all directions. In addition, the gourd will start making much noise. That is what happens to us, too, when we are not filled with the Holy Spirit. We will be going all kinds of places and what people will hear are not the things of God, but other sounds."

O, how they understand the words of our Lord, when He said that the people are hard of hearing! "We do the same things. We have been warned by our teacher. Some of you have been warned by your parents and grandparents. You hear the warnings in God's Book. But we, too, are very often hard of hearing. We know it, but don't act according to what we have heard!" someone would say. "God, provide ears for my heart!" one of them prayed. "God, pierce my heart with your Word!" we heard someone else pray.

They drink in the Word of God as it is taught. The weeks of Bible School every year are a highlight for many. It was great to hear some of those testimonies at the close! The Trio expression for being full after having eaten is: 'I am with stomach!' And that is very often visible. But then they started using this same expression after having been fed with the Word of God. Spiritually well nourished!

"My heart is with stomach!" or, "My head is with stomach!"

In one situation the 'theology' of one of the Indian Bible teachers was not exactly correct. However we did not want to correct him on the spot. He had come to our house to ask about another man who appeared to have a number of physical problems. Trudy had treated him for a number of different things, but he always came back, after several days, with a new complaint. His blood was checked in a hospital in the city. His blood pressure was measured regularly. So many things were considered and looked at, but he would still come back with complaints. During all that time he only occasionally participated in the different activities, but instead he regularly made his complaints known to other people in the church. Trudy did not know what to do, nor did the doctor, who had also checked this man during a visit to the village. Finally this church leader, obviously tired and concerned about all the complaints, came to see us in our house. He wanted to know what was going on, because the church leaders wanted to pray for him, in a very special way. We shared our thoughts very openly with him and even told him that it was altogether possible that this man was just drawing attention to himself or just lazy. The Indian leader then said: "We are going to pray for him. If he gets better, it will mean that he was sick indeed. If he does not get better, it means that he is not sick." This is how convinced they are of the power of God! Or as they say about God being Omnipotent: God is beyond Power!

In another situation, someone came running to our house to tell us that some children in the village were dying. We were not always very concerned when we heard this kind of thing, but the way this news came across to us, we had a good idea that something was drastically wrong. So we went over to the hut where the children were. Indeed, we saw three young children on the ground and more or less lifeless. From what we were told, we learned that they had been playing together and had gotten hold of a gourd and had eaten the inside. These three children usually played together as they were children of three sisters, who lived close to each other. Trudy and I started praying. After all, they were just a little younger than our own children.

We first went to the short-wave radio to contact the doctor so Trudy could ask for advice. After he had heard about the problem he checked himself to see what kind of poison there could have been in that gourd. When he came back on the radio he told us what he had found out. There was the possibility of one of two poisons in that gourd. But those poisons had to be treated differently. "You do have both medications in your clinic," he said, "but I cannot tell you which poison it is and therefore I do not know with which medication you should treat it." The only thing we could do was to ask God to direct Trudy to the right one. In the clinic she picked one of the two medications, and together we returned to the hut where the sick children were.

As we approached the hut, we heard people singing: "God is so good! God is so good!" Would this have been the song we would have chosen, if we had found ourselves in the same situation as these mothers? Once inside the hut we found a number of the church leaders present. After singing another song, one of them suggested quoting from God's Paper: "Be anxious for nothing, but in everything, by prayer and supplication with thanksgiving, let your requests be made known unto God!" (Phil.4:6) Now they were putting into practice the reality of God's Word. It was a thrill to us to hear some of them lead in prayer. Words and thoughts like these were expressed:

"Our Father in heaven, we thank You. You are our Maker, the Maker of our bodies. You also made the trees and the plants. All is Your making. You made these children. And today we want to see Your power again. We have asked You things before and You heard our words. Jesus healed people. He raised children from the dead. When Paul was teaching Your Word, a young man fell out of the house, after he had fallen asleep. You raised him up. You have raised up our sick in the past. We praised You after You answered our talk to You. Now we want to praise You again, after You show Your strength to us in these children. You are the 'One Beyond Power'! We thank You!" Now these are probably not the exact words in the exact order because these prayers were sent up by different people, but this is how they spoke to God.

After Trudy gave these children the shots that we had brought, we went home again. We were perplexed! Such faith by people who, seven years before, did not even know about God and Jesus Christ! They did not know that God is good and did not even possess a small portion of the Bible.

Four Trios, who were always involved in the Bible Camp,
Bible translation and distribution of the Trio Old Testament.
Together with their wives, they conducted Bible Conferences in other villages.
They traveled by plane, canoe and on foot.

Many men went out to gather bundles of palm leaves.

After the simple structure had been put up, these palm
leaves were laid down, and fastened with bush vines.

Teaching from Trio Old Testament and New Testament.
Notes on the board were diligently copied.

Our hut at the Bible Camp, after a rain storm!

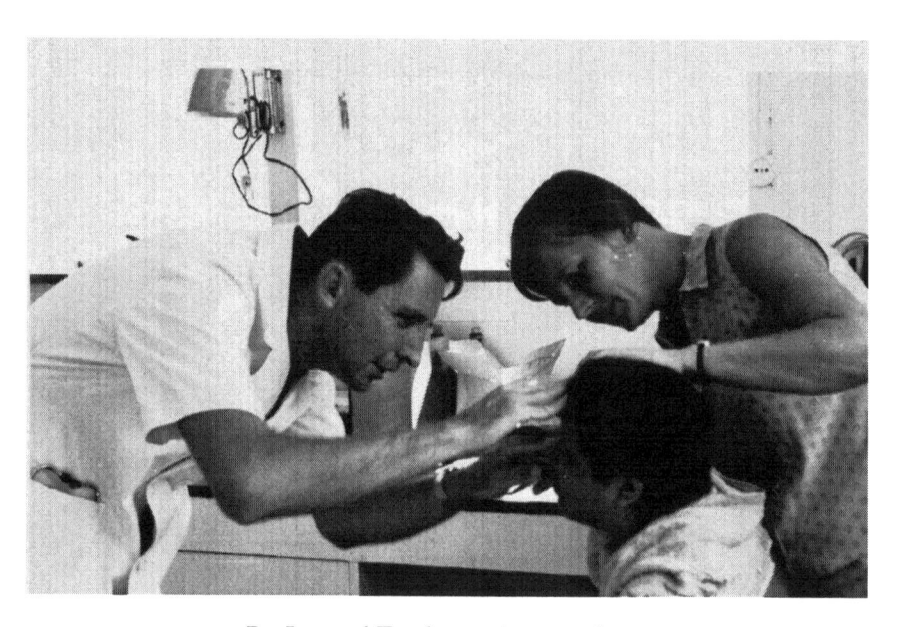

Dr. Jan and Trudy treating a patient.

Trudy with a young man from the Akuriyo tribe, discovered in 1968, when he was just a young boy. Now he is a deacon in one of the Trio churches.

Pastor Hintz and his wife Marilyn, arriving in
Tepoe and on their way to Kënepaku.

Our first night with the Trio Indians, on our way to Apetina, the Wayana village of BIG ARROW.

Trudy's first modern clinic in Tepoe, and our big hut on the left, behind the water tower.

Missionary trip to the coast of Suriname, with twelve Trios.

Clearing in the jungle, where Trios prepared the Akuriyos for village life, during three months. This is where we dropped the food and where the helicopter landed in 1970.

Dedication of newly translated New Testaments in the Trio and Wayana languages, in 1979.

Camp Kënepaku, close to the border with Brazil, where Indians of five or more tribes congregated each year for Bible teaching.

Bible School building with part of the student body and their children. Usually Indians conducted a VBS, and at times there were 250 people present, from three countries.

Pastor Dan Skogen taught from Exodus and constructed a Tabernacle from jungle materials, with the help of a group of students. The last day of his teaching, we took a tour, while Dan did more explaining and teaching.

The different tribal churches grew, as people, after having been disciples, decided to follow Christ and be baptized. One of our special blessings was to see how church leaders of one tribe, baptized members of other tribes.

In 2013 and 2014 the Bible teaching was mainly for the leaders of the Trio churches, as we were getting those churches ready for official incorporation, and the completion of the complete Bible in the Trio language.

The first pulpit at Camp Weejo.

Everyone realized that they would be doing the teaching in their own villages.

Henry Fred Warema Shupiri
1940's 1950's 1960's 1990's

"IN GOING"

Our going ! Their going !

Your going ? A sacrifice ?

"How hear we every man in our own tongue…!" Acts 2:8

Chapter 13

Missionary Trips by and with the Trios

The first mission trip during our time with the Trio Indians was in 1965. They had already made many trips, sometimes up the Tapanahony River but even more times up the Paloemeu River. Many of the Trios had come from the East Paru River region in Brazil. After the first ones had come to Suriname and heard the Gospel, they had the natural desire to let their relatives and people of other tribes know what they had heard. Some of them even returned to the villages where they had lived before being saved themselves. What they had heard in Suriname sounded so good that they wanted others to hear about it as well.

We watched the first group leave for Brazil, going up the Paloemeu River. They were not only interested in reaching people of their own tribe, but in reaching people of many other tribes. In order to find an entrance into those tribes, and into the hearts of those people, they wanted to take gifts to them. It was also a way to show that they had come with good intentions. Money was not all that important to them in those days, as all of them were traders by nature.

On the Sunday before they planned to leave, we had an official send-off for them during the morning service. On Monday they left. It was not normal to arrange trips a long time beforehand. Sometimes they even made arrangements for their departure on the day they were going to leave. Even the canoes had not been chosen yet. But the believers and unbelievers would eventually come to the riverside. And they did show up! Many of them! As they showed up, the villagers brought and piled up their gifts for those who were going to make the trip and for those who were going to be visited: cassava bread, bananas, sweet potatoes, drink, sugarcane, and different kinds of cooked and smoked meat and fish. These were all items for use during the trip on the river and through the jungle. But the travelers also took with them items for those they wanted to reach with the Gospel: beads, red loin cloth, matches, salt, wood for making bows, and arrow cane; some new pots and pans, tripods to put over the fire to cook on, machetes and files and some used and some new axe heads. If they had taken all of it, they would have needed two extra canoes. The villagers were generous, way beyond our expectations!

Trips by regular canoe were very time-consuming. Some of the men had learned to handle an outboard motor mounted on a much larger canoe. This saved time, and therefore also food, for the trip. But the fuel for the motor had to be purchased, of course. Just think about carrying everything across the mountain range between Suriname and Brazil!

Gradually more money was being introduced into the tribe, which was used instead of barter in some cases. Some people were able to work for different government departments. Others made some money by making Indian artifacts, items they used and still use themselves: bows and arrows, Indian combs, beadwork, decorations made with feathers and beautiful pottery. These things we sold for them to visiting tourists and to souvenir shops in the city of Paramaribo.

When the Trios began to ask questions about giving money to God, they wanted to know how the Israelites used to give. That is when we introduced the matter of tithing. Another difficulty! People who had previously had no concept of numbers had no idea either of the term 'percent.' They were used to counting to three: single, double and uneven; and they counted with their fingers. If it went beyond uneven, they had to put two fingers together: two singles, two doubles, two times 'uneven' and then four doubles and five doubles. Each time putting two fingers together, but they really did not have words for those numbers; they could only show what they meant with their fingers. If it was more than that, they used to just point at their feet as well. How were we going to help them understand the idea of ten percent? They did get Suriname money and saw the numbers on the bills. The only value they attached to that money, in the beginning, was what they could buy with it. A one-guilder bill would give them one yard of red loincloth or one pound of salt. Making a bow and five arrows of a certain size would give them the money to buy a certain amount of red cloth, or an aluminum pot or some kerosene, etc.

The Trios asked me to write down how much they could give for the Lord's work, and the money they put in God's Box, which was kept in the church building. The list was made and copies of it were put up in different places, even in our house. It worked for a good number of them, but for others it was too complicated. We remember the time when one of the men came into the house with a twenty-five-guilder bill. He had done some work for outsiders and wanted to contribute to the Lord's work. I took him over to the list, trying to explain the system used by the people in Moses' time and thereafter. For ten, you give one to the Lord, and for twenty you give two and for thirty you give three. But twenty-five is not twenty and not thirty either. It is right in between. What do we do now? Then the question came, which we will never forget: "Will God be unhappy with me if I give fifteen of the twenty-five to Him?"

In the years that followed, the Trios financed many of their own missionary trips to different places and tribes. They made trips not only to Brazil, but also to French Guyana and to the coast of Suriname.

They became very much involved in reaching a stone-age tribe called the Akudiyos. God opened the door to these people, quite unexpectedly, in 1968, when some Wayana Indians returning from delivering building materials to a location near the border with Brazil, decided to do some fishing. They stopped their outboard motors and just drifted down the river, while casting their hooks and lines in the water. It was at that time that they heard some noises in the jungle. At first, they thought they had heard wild pigs, but when they landed on the bank of the river, they came face to face with a small group from the Akudiyo tribe instead.

Many more trips were made and many more small groups of the same tribe were found. Being a nomadic tribe, moving about in the jungles of Suriname, the Akudiyos had no village, just small temporary shelters, and their hammocks were made from sisal. Often children slept under fallen trees.

Ivan and Doris Schoen especially, together with some of our mutual colleagues, made many trips to reach the people of this tribe, always assisted by believing Trios and Wayanas. Later on, during our time, they were assisted by Art and Evy Yohner.

Morgan and I made one trip, together with the Indian believers from Tepoe. It actually was the longest separation for Trudy and me from one another since we got married. The whole trip lasted one month and included our sixth wedding anniversary. After leaving Tepoe, Morgan and I went down the Tapanahony River until we reached Stoelman's Island on the east side of Suriname, bordering French Guyana. From there we followed the Marowijne River, which changes name as you go south, upriver.

The trip was quite uneventful until we were just a few hours away from the Wayana mission station, on the Lawa River. The motor ran well and the sound of it was rather monotonous. But suddenly our canoe ran aground on a submerged rock. The rock was not visible, because the water covered it, and it was pretty pointed. Then my foot came up and the rock came through the bottom of the dugout. The water gushed in. I managed to push the loose piece of wood back down again with my foot, so there was less water coming in, but it still took two men to bail the water out of the canoe for the next three hours. Then we arrived at the Wayana village of Kawemhakan, and several men repaired the canoe, so we could leave again the next morning.

We followed the border-river almost all the way to the border with Brazil. That was the area where the Akudiyos had last been seen. All of us began our journey through the jungle: up a hill and down a hill, through creeks and swamps. We were not walking very fast, as Morgan was having trouble keeping up. I heard some of the men, behind me, talk about the slowness of the whole group. Then they began to pass me and started walking faster. I adopted the faster speed and kept up with them. So now we were two parties. Some of the hills were very steep and the pressure in my ears began to increase. "That is what happens when a white man travels through the jungle like an Indian!" I thought. But a few minutes later I heard the Trios complain about the same thing. It made me feel a lot better. A few hours later our group reached an old Akudiyo camp and we decided that it was going to be the end of our journey that day. It was hours later when the other group came struggling up the mountain. When I saw Morgan, I said: "You look like a ghost!" not ever having seen one. He answered: "I think I feel like one!"

In order to take a bath, we had to go down a steep hill to a mountain creek. The water was quite cold, as there was never any sunshine under all those trees.

The next morning the Trios decided that two of them would search out the area, looking for camps made by these stone-age people. Their camps were usually only about a two-hour walk apart, for us. When there was nothing else to eat in one place, the Akudiyos moved to the next temporary location. The trail these nomadic Indians followed was never a straight one. Therefore it was possible that they had made a circle and so could still be close to where we had made our camp. After two days these two members of our party returned to the camp and told us that they had followed the trail to camp number twenty-three. "That means," they said, "that they are closer to the Oelemarie River, west of us, than to the Litani River we are on now!"

It would not be wise to follow them through the jungle with all our gear. Therefore, after consulting by radio with Ivan in the village of Big Arrow, the decision was made to go down the Litani River and then go up the Oelemarie River.

Going . . . ! A Sacrifice?

During our first night on an island in that river, the rain started to come down. First it rained lightly, but soon it became a downpour. Some of the Indians spent part of the night making sure our canoe would not fill up with water. All of our belongings, including our food and fuel, were in it, and even our short-wave receiver and transmitter, with antenna plus battery. By five o'clock in the morning I woke up when Sikoi told me that the canoe was gone. The Indians had fallen asleep too!

"What do we do now?" Sikoi said. "Go and find it!" was my answer. No reason for all of us to start looking. Staying dry in our hammocks and praying out loud would be more productive.

Finding their way through the jungle near the river, Sikoi and another man did locate the canoe, stuck in the branches and fortunately on our side of the river. By seven o'clock they were back on our island.

Eating breakfast did not take long and in the meantime it had stopped raining. We continued our trip upstream and found the place from which, according to our map, we should start looking for the elusive Akudiyos. Again a number of our team went out to start looking. They promised to be back in two days. But that night it started to rain again. We all had little fires going in our huts, because we had heard jaguars close to our huts. The river began to flood, however, and every so often we could hear a not-so-welcome sound. It was the typical 'dialogue' between water and fire. All we could do was to get up and tie up our hammocks, so that the mosquito nets would not reach into the water. We were under the trees, about fifty yards away from the river. Fortunately, it did eventually get light again, although the rain continued. The river was really swollen and the canoe was brought to each hut. We got out of our hammocks, untied those hammocks and put them in the canoe. Once everybody had been rescued, we left that camp as well, to find some spot where we could expect to stay dry, even if the river should rise a lot more.

We found that spot. It was near one of the towers which were used for the project of making a new map of the country. The people who had used the camp had left a small canoe behind, probably for future use.

In thinking about the men who had left on the trail the day before, it was decided to take that small canoe to the last camp and leave a note for them, telling them where we were.

They could use the canoe to come to our camp.

It was now Sunday. We held a simple service: sang together, prayed together and I shared from the Word. Since it was still early, I suggested that I would take the canoe to the camp from the night before. At exactly noon some of the men would come with the big canoe and outboard motor to pick me up. It was a wonderful boat ride in between those big trees and through an area that had really flooded, because of all the rain. The riverbanks could not be seen anymore. Then I heard a sound, like somebody cutting a tree.

As I approached the ever clearer sound, I wondered if this could be one of those Akudiyo Indians, maybe trying to cut honey out of a tree with his stone axe. At times the sound would stop and then start up again. First softly, then louder. I really wasn't all that anxious to meet those stone-age people all by myself. After all, the first encounters between them and other Indians and missionaries had not been very friendly. As I kept going downstream in the swift running water, the sound became weaker. It was really too rhythmic to think that it was someone cutting a tree. But you never know!

Close to noon I arrived at my destination and it was shortly thereafter that I heard the motorboat in the distance. When Pisere and some others arrived, I shared with them what I had heard. I asked the motor man to let me run the motor to the place where I had heard the sound. Arriving there, I stopped the motor and all of us could clearly hear what I had heard before. An investigation showed that it was one of those bush vines which, because of the heavy rains, was under the surface of the water. The water pushed it up and then it swung back and hit a tree just under the water surface. Problem solved!

But I still ended up causing more problems. Instead of turning the motor over to Pisere again, who was the official motor man, I decided to continue to run it. Not for long, though! At a certain moment I saw some of the Indians, in front of me, move their hands up in the air and subconsciously I must have noticed something approaching my face too. Before I knew it, I was pulled over the motor, when another vine was under my elbow and my arm in front of my face. I landed in the water, while the boat just kept going. There was no way for me to swim upstream. The water was too powerful, so I started to float downstream, keeping an eye on the canoe. Pisere reacted quickly and ran through the canoe to the motor at the back and proceeded to put it in reverse to come and pick me up. It was not possible to turn the canoe around, because there was no room in the river to do that. I am sure it took only a minute or two, at the most, for the boat to reach me, but it felt like half an hour. All that went through my mind was: ALLIGATORS! I had heard that they would not attack a person standing up in the water, but that they will attack a person who is swimming. I was pulled back into the canoe by several Indians, and we reached our own camp safely.

Just sitting in my hammock the rest of that Sunday afternoon did not appeal to me. So I asked some of the men if they felt like climbing the mountain, behind our camp, where a 75-foot high tower was located. They liked that idea, too. Once we had reached the tower, it looked inviting to us to climb it. We decided to accept the challenge. Two of the men went first, then I followed, and a third Indian followed me. When we were about twenty feet from the top, the Indian who was right above me, the second person from the top, decided that the height was not for him. How he got past me, I have no idea. The ladder was pretty narrow. Three of us reached the top and I was able to take some slides of the Suriname jungle north of us, and the mountains south of us, in Brazil.

Later that afternoon, after we got back to our huts and after we took a bath in the river, Pisere came over to my hammock. He wanted to talk with me. "Why did you do these three bad things today?" he asked.

At first, I did not know what he was talking about, but he was going to give me a piece of his mind. First of all, I had had the courage to take that canoe all by myself to the camp downstream. Secondly, I had taken his responsibility from him, by handling the outboard motor myself. He had been appointed by the Tepoe church to be the motor man! Thirdly, I had climbed that tower and asked other Indians to go with me. Now I knew that Pisere was afraid of heights, but that is not why he brought this up. He said: "Three times today you could have caused us trouble. If anything had happened to you or to the Trios with you, I would have been held accountable by the people of my tribe!" He was right! The events of the day and my correction by a brother in the Lord changed much of our thinking and were of much help to both Trudy and me in the years to follow.

The Trios encouraged the Akudiyos to settle down in one place and taught them many things — not only about God and what Jesus Christ had done for them, but many other things. Some of the Trios began to live among the Akudiyo people, who numbered only about seventy at that time. In order to keep them in the same place, food needed to be provided for them. They could hunt and fish, but the area around them was soon depleted of nuts and fruits and roots, which were a substantial part of their diet.

Soon people from this nomadic tribe expressed a desire to live with the Trios in their village. That is where the food was! After a period of time, the Akudiyos seemed to be ready for the change from nomadic life to village life. Some of them had already been moved to Tepoe, by canoe and mission Cessna. For all of them it was a new experience. They had never been in a canoe. Airplanes they had heard above the jungle, and some of them had seen one before. All of them saw the mission plane as we dropped hundreds of pounds of cassava to them from the air, into an area which they had cleared in the jungle. The pilot flew the plane over a hill close by and quickly descended to the open area in the jungle. I had time to push two or three bags or baskets of food out of the plane, from which the cargo door had been removed. We kept doing this until all the food had been dropped.

Now, for the move of all of them to Tepoe, we were offered help by KLM Aerocarto. They were making a new map of the country. Indians were employed by that company to move materials to places deep in the jungle. For this project of making a new map, towers were needed in many places. Once the towers were built, surveys were done from an airplane and crews were moved by helicopter from one location to the next one.

The person in charge of the KLM project in the jungle wondered how help could be given to the Indians and to us. The large Heliswiss helicopter could take many of them on just one flight. On one of the MAF flights we saw how a total of sixteen of the small Indians and children were being brought to our village. It was quite interesting to see how they were packed into all corners of that small Cessna plane. They wanted to go together as a group and, since weight allowed it, the pilot decided to bring them all at the same time.

Together with the Trio believers, the Akudiyos had cleared an area near their camp, where the helicopter could land. For months they had lived in that area. The trees had only been cut in the beginning. It allowed us to drop the necessary food to them, from the MAF Cessna. But now some of the tree stumps had been removed as well. I flew from Tepoe to the clearing on the first shuttle, to help organize the flights to Tepoe. Trudy and Dr. Jan were at Tepoe to welcome the 'immigrants'. All of them needed a thorough medical check-up and some shots. The men in the village had built many new huts, and families had been assigned to assist the ones coming to live with them.

None of the Akudiyos had ever lived in a village situation before. They had many things to learn – preparing food, bathing themselves, cleaning their huts, and many more things. The Trios and Wayanas provided such a wonderful and warm Christian welcome for these stone-age people! The Akudiyos had never seen many of the items which they now encountered in the village.

All of them rejoiced in what they saw and experienced. But for a couple of those in the group, life came to an early end. The health of some of them was not the best. They had already been sick while they were in the jungle. The idea of being cared for may have kept some alive until they reached Tepoe. Some of them were children born from a union between father and daughter, or brother and sister. "We knew we were finishing ourselves by living this way, but we continued in it anyway!" one of them said. Soon two of them refused all food and told all of us that they wanted to die. This was something others had practiced when they were in the jungle. Once they got word that one of the older persons in the tribe had died, the next oldest person would take off into the jungle by himself, without taking any fire with him. He or she decided that they were next in line to die.

When the small groups met each other during the course of the year, they would share the news that a certain person's fire had gone out. Each group always carried a piece of burning firewood with them. Literally and figuratively, their fires had gone out! Even during the last weeks of these people's lives, the Trios and Wayanas at Tepoe continued to care for them and to share the good news of their Creator and the Lord Jesus Christ. When one of them finally understood the message of God's saving grace, his physical strength was so far gone that death followed anyway.

That is how the Akudiyos were reached. Nowadays, some of that tribe are involved in reaching other tribes for Christ, and some have become deacons in their local churches.

It was 1971. The Tepoe believers had made many trips across the borders, to share their faith with people of other tribes, but there are other Amerindian tribes near the coast of Suriname. The Caribs are there and the Arowaks. The Tepoe believers began to talk about their desire to visit these tribes as well. Arrangements were made with a missionary on the Marowijne River in Albina. It was about a five-day river trip, down the Tapanahony River to Stoelman's Island again. There the river flows into the Marowijne River, which is the border between Suriname and French Guyana, in northern Suriname.

We were able to take a full forty-five foot canoe with a twenty- horsepower motor on it. Our team consisted of thirteen members. One of the men was a church leader from the larger Trio church in the village of Alalapadu. We went over the same waterfalls and through the same rapids which Trudy and I had passed on our first river trip with the Trios. This time we had a few more problems than before. As soon as we arrived at the first falls, we noticed that the wind had blown down a sizeable tree and it had landed on the rocks, right where we had planned to drag the canoe to the other side of the falls. It took us hours to clear a trail over which we could bring the canoe to the right spot. We used axes and machetes and together we moved the branches. When we were pulling the canoe over the rocks of the third falls, we suddenly heard the bottom of our canoe crack. "Satan may not want us to go on this trip!" one of the Trios said. That was probably true. Fortunately there are supports in such big canoes, so the damage was limited. However, after we pushed the canoe back in the water, we noticed that it was leaking in a bad way. We had still more traveling to do before we reached the next village. And there were a few more waterfalls to cross as well.

After several hours we reached the Wayana village of Big Arrow, where Trudy and I had begun our ministry among Indians, in 1965. Pieces of metal roofing were found and some old pieces of cloth and nails. Our team members spent hours fixing the motor boat and were successful in doing so. Later that afternoon we went on our way again and spent the night in a Bushnegro village.

Further down the river, a couple of days later we came to the place called 'Three Islands'. It is still not clear to us why only three. The river is pretty wide there and there are many islands. The Indians, having made the trip before, knew exactly which channel to go through and between which islands. When we came to the largest waterfall on this trip, we used some small railroad cars on which to put the canoe and our luggage and fuel. Taking everything on the tracks down the hill was easy, but when we returned at the end of the month, we faced another problem, as you can imagine.

On our way home, we would be going uphill!

The rest of the boat trip was pretty uneventful. We did have some bailing to do, to keep the water out of our canoe, but there were no more waterfalls. Only when we got closer to Albina and St. Laurent did we find out that our canoe was not made for that kind of river. We were closer to the coast now and the river was wide and the water quite choppy. The wind created the kind of waves that our canoe was not made for. In order to visit the different Indian villages, which were even further downstream, we were able to use other boats, which were actually made for that kind of water.

We all spent the nights in and under the house of our missionary colleague, Rob Sussenbach. The days that followed were spent in visiting a number of villages. Tamenta, the former Trio witchdoctor, had made the trip with us. Not easy for a man who had the use of only one leg! When we first met him, he walked on two hands and one foot. The paralyzed leg was tied up with a string, that is, the ankle was tied to his thigh. We had been able to get crutches for him, but during the trip he had gone back to his old way of moving. Later on, he was able to use his crutches again, most of the time.

Going . . . ! A Sacrifice?

After entering a village, we were always directed to the meeting hut. Most villages have one, because that is where business is discussed. Some of the team members would do the introduction: who we were, and where we had come from, how long it had taken us to get to the village and that everyone in our village was doing well. Someone from the host village would then reply, by letting us know that all were well in his village, or that some were sick, or that the village owner was away.

Then Tamenta would begin talking to those present. In the normal Trio way, he would look around the circle, without actually looking the people in the face. Before too long, he was talking to just one individual. That one responded, either by mumbled words or by nodding his head. Later on I found out that the men who responded that way to Tamenta were the witchdoctors of the villages.

I still don't know how Tamenta knew that these men were witchdoctors,

Many villages were visited during those days. In the meantime we had acquired company. A television crew had come to Suriname to make some missionary films, for broadcasting in the Netherlands. They knew my name, but did not know that we were so close to the coast. God directed them to our team in an amazing way. Quite a few of the meetings in the villages were filmed.

The Trios were interested in visiting other Indian villages, on a different river, farther west of the city of Paramaribo. That meant that we had to get on those 'wild buses' and make the trip to Paramaribo, by way of Moengo. From Paramaribo we could use the same kind of transportation to the next river. The road to that river follows the northern coast of Suriname. Once, after we had reached our destination by bus, we were able to rent a large canoe and outboard motor.

The reception in the villages we visited was quite different from what we had experienced on the Marowijne River. People were not interested; many were even antagonistic and very cold. In several villages, we were not even welcome to go on shore. That was quite discouraging. We could not even sow the seed. But what would happen to the seed which we had been able to sow in the other villages?

It was not until 1992 that we received an answer to that question. In that year we had to make a trip from Paramaribo to Albina. Christian friends suggested that we make that trip together in their car. That way we could be back on the same day. The following morning we needed to get on the mission plane to go to Tepoe. We met Rob, the missionary with whom we had visited the villages in 1971. He and some others were involved in training some nationals for the Lord's work. As we visited his home, he introduced Trudy and me to some of the people. When we came to an older Indian man, he asked us: "Do you remember him?" No, I sure did not! Then he told us that he was the witchdoctor in one of the villages we had visited years before.

At some point after our visit he had come to a saving knowledge of Jesus Christ and had immediately abandoned his witchcraft.

What a privilege to see some spiritual fruit after so many years!

We needed to return to Tepoe. However, in the meantime the television crew, of which there were only two men left, wanted to go to Tepoe as well. They certainly would not fit in our canoe, especially since they had all their equipment with them. Contact was made by radio with Trudy, who had stayed behind with Rosyanne and Artwin. She was able to arrange for another canoe to make the trip from Tepoe to Stoelman's Island. The television crew would return to Paramaribo by car and charter a plane to that village. We would go there by boat. During the days together with these two men, I had learned some things about them. The cameraman had some months before come to know the Lord. He had spent many years in producing films of a quite different genre. Now, after having been saved, he wanted to serve his Lord. The other man, the producer, was not saved. Listening to what he had to say, and listening to his questions, I thought that he knew the Lord. Later on I found out that I had been wrong in my conclusion. He told me himself when we met again to begin our six-day canoe trip to Tepoe. They left that same day by car, and we left a few days later by canoe. The Indians coming from Tepoe to meet us at Stoelman's Island had left, too. Their trip was going to be a fast one, since they had only their hammocks and some food with them.

We did not know that the rains had started in the south of Suriname. We were still enjoying sunshine and dry weather near the coast. But when we had traveled for a day or so, we could tell that the river was up considerably. The next morning we changed the propeller on our motor. A new one would do better than the one we had been using. We noticed that some areas, where people had huts, were flooded.

On our way downstream, we had made arrangements to buy fuel for our motor and when we reached that small village, we saw immediately that much of it was under water. We took the boat as far as we could, so we would not have to haul the fifty-five gallon drum too far through the water. All went well until we tried to leave. Our motor man started the motor and put it in reverse. But our canoe did not move. We got out of the boat and pushed it a little bit and noticed that it was not stuck, so he tried to move it again by using the motor. It made a lot of noise, but the boat did not move.

We had lost our new propeller!

At first nobody was very concerned, because we still had the old propeller. But then it hit us: we had lost washers and nuts as well, which attached the prop to the foot of the motor. That was more serious! Apparently the new prop had not been fastened securely enough and I had never thought about checking it. Since the motor had been running all the time we were on the river, it had stayed on. But when we slowed down to pick up the fuel, we had lost that new and expensive prop. Nobody on the river had that kind of motor. All those who owned a motor had different brands. We were stuck! All we could do was pray!

Our fuel provider was willing to put his motor on our canoe and tie a small boat behind it. He would bring us to the next village, of over one hundred inhabitants. He was sure that somebody there would be able to help us. We continued our trip, after having lost several hours; and our speed was not that great, since we had a smaller motor and an extra canoe to pull.

In the next village we found several men who were willing to help, but nobody had parts for our motor, nor the tools. The Indians negotiated for hours with our Bushnegro friends. All we could do was to spend the night in their village with the promise that they would see what they could do the next day.

Early the next day our hosts for the night offered to pull our canoe to Stoelman's Island. At the jungle hospital there, we might be able to find parts. We left right away, but the traveling was even slower than the day before. Now it was a big canoe and a small motor, towing our forty-five foot boat with thirteen people in it, and all our gear, plus drums and cans filled with fuel.

Fortunately, it was not raining.

Early that afternoon we arrived at our destination and were met by the two television men. They had been waiting more than two days and of course had no idea why we did not show up sooner.

An investigation showed that nobody there would be able to help with the parts we needed. There were lots of parts for the motors of other brands, but nothing for ours. Boxes of the other parts were brought to our canoe, and our cameraman began his work. He had never worked on an outboard motor in his whole life, but he prayed and we prayed. While the Indians sang their Christian songs, he sang or whistled various hymns. "Praise the Lord, it is going to work!' he said from time to time. Hours passed. It was now late afternoon. "Don't worry, God is going to do this for us!" he said more than once. In the meantime, we had contacted Paramaribo by radio and told them what had happened. One of the mission pilots was going to buy all the necessary parts and they would be dropped in the river somewhere on our way. "I am done! This is going to work!" our mechanic exclaimed. You should have seen the contraption this man had built on the foot of our motor! The factory would have been ashamed of it, but we were filled with joy.

The willing helpers in the city were quickly informed by radio not to drop the requested parts to us, but to leave them at the village of Big Arrow instead. We expected to be there several days later. However, we never needed to put that new prop on the motor until we reached Tepoe. The contraption to hold the old prop on worked the whole way.

We could still travel at least one hour and make it to one of the villages, below the first waterfalls. The people welcomed us to their village and showed us some beautiful clean huts. After we had eaten and put up our hammocks, everybody was ready to go to sleep — all except our film producer. "Pastor," he said, "now you preach!" I was surprised and my face must have shown it! "Yes, you may think that I am born again, but I am not. I know the language, I have the right questions, and even the answers, but I am not a Christian!" he said.

My mind went into the fastest gear.

Well, if he asked for it, I would give it to him, with all barrels. If he was not a Christian, then he was a heathen, and I started reading from the book of Romans chapter one. 'They are without excuse.' 'They knew God, but they glorified Him not as God.' 'They did all kinds of things…' "Yes, but..!" he said. And the excuses came. 'Thou art inexcusable!' 'All have sinned and come short…!' My 'preaching' lasted a long time. Some of our group must have gone to sleep. It was not in their language anyway. 'For God so loved the world, that He gave His only begotten Son, that whosoever believeth in Him, should not perish, but have everlasting life.' This was the same message we had shared with the Indians at Tepoe and now in all the Indian villages which we had just visited. Would it bear fruit?

Weeks later, we received word from someone at the broadcasting office that our inquisitive fellow traveler had returned to the office. The first day, when he and his colleagues started their work with a time of devotions and prayer, this man testified of his faith in Jesus Christ. All he had heard, as well as his having seen the changed lives of the Tepoe believers, had impressed him and had helped him accept His Savior. It was not until much later that we received the news that he had passed away from cancer, which he had already been suffering from when we were together. He had never mentioned it to me.

We must have had too much excitement on our trip, because the rest of our voyage was pretty dull — until we arrived at one of the last waterfalls. Going through the rapids near Three Islands was quite a chore. We were going uphill with those little wagons, on those rails.

After a couple of days we reached those waterfalls again, about six of them or so, just upriver from Big Arrow. We had taken most of our belongings out of the canoe, and were able to advance the boat close to the first rock formation. However, the river was still rising. It was only a matter of one second and probably only one wave, coming over a rock. Our big canoe scooped up water and filled up before our eyes in a matter of just seconds. Fortunately, the expensive camera equipment had been taken out of the boat already and all our hammocks as well. Just a few unimportant items were missing when we took inventory.

"BUT these are written...." John 20:31

Chapter 14

"Write a book!" many said

The Bible verse in the heading deals, of course, with what the Apostle John wrote about the life of Christ. John's purpose in writing his Gospel was 'that *the world* might believe that Jesus is the Christ, the Son of God; and that believing *mankind* might have life through His name.'

We have written this book in order to encourage people, young and old, to get more involved in missions. We hope that it will bring a renewed vision for the missionary endeavor into churches. There are many who have not heard. Many have not been reached with the glorious Gospel of Jesus Christ:

HIS DEATH - HIS BURIAL - HIS RESURRECTION
1 Corinthians 15:3-4

For many years, various supporters and friends have been telling us that we should write down the stories we told them, but we have never shared all the stories and experiences. Many people have asked us questions during meetings and after meetings in churches, or in their homes. When we answered those questions, there was often much surprise. Then, some said again: "Why don't you write a book?" Our answer has always been: "How will we find the time to write? The most important thing for us now is to get the translation of the Bible, in the Trio language, finished!"

But then a good number of them answered: "It is very important for other people to learn about your missionary life. Who else but you can share these events with generations to come? People have no idea about what you have experienced and what life is like on a mission field like yours!"

After finishing the translation of the Old Testament, and completing the revision of the Trio New Testament in November 2016, we started thinking again about doing something with our stories. We had quite a bit in the computer already, starting in the 1990's. Five different people offered to edit those stories, but each one handed us back the files we had, after reading the manuscript. We are sure it is a lot of work!! But finally one lady, in a supporting church in Indiana, offered to do this work for us. She had done a lot of editing previously. We are grateful to her!!

So now we have decided to put some more of these stories on paper. It is our desire that God will somehow use it all for His Glory!

While thinking about a title for this book, many things have come to our minds, such as:

Go Ye into All the World!
or:
Make Our Church Great Again!

Does that remind you of something?

Right now, as we are working on these stories, we hear about the military in this country — not really what it used to be. We wonder if Trudy and I would have been liberated in the Netherlands if the military force of the United States of America at that time had been what it is now. Actually, as someone else has stated: We might all be speaking Russian or German now.

Isn't it the same with the missionary force in our day? We think of the stories we have read about pioneer missionaries from long ago.

They went out, just trusting the Lord to supply their every need. Furloughs were not thought of. They were just giving their lives, so that others might hear about Eternal Life.

But we also think of the men and their wives who, shortly after WWII, came back to Europe. Many had fought in the military, and now were accompanied by others who caught the vision. Europe was a needy continent, where Christianity had once been strong and the churches and individuals on that continent eventually influenced churches and groups in the US to become strong 'mission sending agencies'!

But then a different title came to our minds. And that is the one we put on the cover of this book: **IN GOING...! A Sacrifice?** The reasons we chose this title are many. The Great Commission, as we call it in Matthew 28, is usually translated "GO YE..." The actual wording is: "**IN GOING...**" To me, that is even stronger than the imperative in the English language and other languages.

Let me explain: When I went to high school in the Netherlands, that school was about six or seven miles away from where we lived. There were times when my mother wanted something from a store in that city. She would say: "On your way home this afternoon, buy this or that for me! She mentioned the item and the store that had it, and she gave me the money to purchase it. You see, she did not order me to come home in the afternoon. It was just expected that I would come home. But 'while I was coming home', I needed to do something. That is how we see the Great Commission: "Making Disciples, While Going into All the World!'

Too often, as we had the privilege of sharing our ministries in different churches and in home meetings, we heard the word:

SACRIFICE

Pastors often introduced us to their pulpit with those words and then talked about how much we had sacrificed in going where we have gone. If a pastor dwelt too long on that theme, it felt as though he was taking the wind out of our sails. How could we glorify the Lord in sharing how He had been working, when we were being praised for our sacrifice?

We have shared many times that there is no sacrifice involved for us. Romans 12: 1 mentions: "...present your bodies a living sacrifice... which is your reasonable service." Maybe there should be more emphasis on that truth while reaching people for the Lord, and seeing them make decisions as far as salvation is concerned. The aspect of salvation and 'making that sacrifice of "presenting yourselves..."' should be taught as well. Once the sacrifice from that verse has been made, there are no other sacrifices to be made.

From that point on, everything we are, everything we do, and everything we have, is the natural result of that initial sacrifice, a living sacrifice. And if people make that sacrifice, it is simply the result of the Ultimate Sacrifice our Lord made.

When the Trios were taught these truths in the book of Romans, we soon thereafter heard them say: "What good is a dead sacrifice to Jesus? While we are alive we are of value for Jesus!" Do you get it? There is nothing else to give up for the Lord, when we have given it ALL to HIM.

As we shared some of the experiences written about in this book, others would come to us afterwards and say: "I could never do what you did there in the jungle! I saw and heard how you live there with these people, without all the comforts we are used to here. I would not be able to do it!"

"How can you say that you would never be able to do it, if you haven't even tried, or given it any consideration?" was our answer. It is like many children who say that they do not like a certain food, without ever having tried it. There are plenty of excuses in the Word of God of people who tell the Lord that they couldn't do it.

Another thing that has bothered us at times is parents who have dedicated their baby to the Lord, enjoying *(or not enjoying)* the way that baby grows up, but when that child has become a teenager, those parents and their teenagers have made up their minds already about what the future will be. "Just the thought of my children being so far away!" "Not seeing our grandchildren grow up...." "We are a close family and those thoughts scare us!" were some of the comments we heard about the prospect of mission service by their children.

Sure, my parents would have preferred to see us stay close. Sure, they wanted our children, their grandchildren, to be within reach. Sure, we came to the point that we had to leave our children behind and also our grandchildren. Being able to see them all the time was more appealing to us, too. But the experience for us of watching our children accept the Lord was the most exhilarating experience we could have had! And we often said: "Now that they know the Lord, there is all eternity to enjoy together!" O, how desirous we can be, as believers, to hold on to the temporary! How much better to be 'laying up treasures in heaven'!

For us, from the beginning, we wanted to see our children come to a personal faith in Jesus Christ. That is what you want as parents when you dedicate your children. It is a wonderful thing to see the Lord answer such prayers for your children. But the next thing we could do is to start praying for our grandchildren. How wonderful to hear the news, from your own children, when their children made that decision and came to personally know the Lord as their Savior!

It is also a wonderful thing to see boys and girls and parents make a decision to obey the Lord. But it is easy to concentrate on the world around you in the ministry God has given you, while neglecting the children God has given to you. On one of our trips as a family, a young lady came to talk to us. It was obvious that she was hurting. She had watched us as a family. Then she shared with us that her parents were in the ministry, too. They worked with children, but then she shared with us: "My parents spend all their time with other children, but they seem to have no time for me!" Hearing these words hurt us deeply, and sent a message to both Trudy and me. This was something we had to watch for and avoid.

The reason why, after eight years, we left the jungle was that we noticed that our children's knowledge of both Dutch and English was limited. When they spent time with other children, while we were in the city of Paramaribo, they would often ask us what a certain word meant. During our linguistics training, it was pointed out that the average person uses on a daily basis a vocabulary of only about eight hundred words. So, if children learn to speak only from their parents, their vocabulary may be limited. Many people know more words, although they may not use all the words they know. Contact with other children and adults increases the vocabulary of children as they are growing up.

As we were faced with these facts, we realized at the same time that God's first institution was Marriage and the Family. The Church came later. For us there were other places where we could serve the Lord and fulfill the Great Commandment.

Look what happened! Many years later, twenty to be exact, the Lord allowed us to return to these Indians in Suriname and finish that ministry. The translation of the Bible is finished and the two Trio Churches in the villages of Tepoe and Paloemeu were officially incorporated in 2016.

"There is joy in serving Jesus," goes the song. The joy is there when bearing fruit and seeing that fruit, just as there is joy when you can see fruit in your own life, and others see it, too.

We did not go out of necessity, but out of gratitude! We have so many reasons to be grateful to God. Let me list them:

1. The Netherlands was liberated by American forces at the end of World War II.

2. The Gospel was brought back to Europe by American missionaries, after that war.

3. Other American WWII fighters came back to Europe as missionaries, to train Europeans for the missionary endeavor in different countries, under American boards. And American churches have supported us for more than fifty-four years.

Our lives are filled with gratitude. As you read this, we just want you to know that this same gratitude can be yours, as you decide to "present your bodies a living sacrifice...which is your reasonable service"!

We lived in very primitive circumstances, but neither one of us ever thought about it as being unduly hard or difficult. Our desire was to serve the Lord and that is what we were doing, because we knew the Lord was the One who wanted us to be there. We had the privilege of seeing the Lord and the Word of God at work. His blessings were innumerable and immeasurable, as we had the great privilege of serving Him, for so long and in many different places. Of course, there were experiences that made us sad as well. There were problems, discouragements and disappointments, as well as triumphs.

We remember the time when one of our neighbors, in the village of Tepoe, came to us early in the morning to tell us that he was going back to his old village, because he was going to work for a company to earn money. He was getting away from the Word at the same time. When we asked him about his relationship with Jesus, he answered: "When I come back after three months, I want to learn more about Him. Then I will accept Him. But now I want the money, so I can buy all these things, like a shotgun and pots and pans!"

We saw him leave that morning. That night, or before daybreak, while we were still in bed, we heard an outboard motor coming from downriver. Normally, Indians do not travel in the dark, and visitors were never welcome after dark. Soon there was a call at our door: "Mother! Can you come? My husband does not wake up!" We went over to the hut, and there he was – the same man who had left in the morning. He was not just asleep; he had already died. Shortly after he began his work, a heavy machine had fallen off a cart. He had tried to keep it from falling on the ground, but was crushed by it. Postponement! "When I come back, I will...!" he had said to us.

Before we tell you more about the ministry in which we were involved, we should tell you a little about ourselves.

Trudy will go first:

"I was born in Amsterdam, before World War II. My father was a tailor. I was the youngest of four children; I had two older sisters and an older brother. When I was a little girl, our whole family moved to the center of the Netherlands. In 1944 the Germans drafted all men up to the age of forty-five. My father was forty-nine and could stay home, but not much later, without any warning, the age limit was raised and those older than forty-five were picked up from the streets. Many of these men were simply going to work, not knowing about the new rules. My dad was picked up as well, as he was on his way to work. A kind lady, who knew our family, quickly came to warn my mom, and told her where all the men had been assembled by the German soldiers. It was a quick trip for all six of us to that street. After waiting and watching so many men marching off, someone told us that there were men on the other side of the block of houses as well, in a street that ran parallel to the one we were on.

"My sisters quickly took the food and other things that my mother had prepared and packed in my little bag. They ran faster than we could. They did see my dad and were able to give him the package. I never saw my dad. He was gone when we reached that street. Then the hard times started. No income, and food was also scarce in those days. My sisters would go out at times and try to find food at farms and other places. They rode bicycles that had rubber or wooden tires, as the Germans had confiscated all bikes that had inflatable tires. Finally, one evening, when it was already dark, there was a knock on the door. My dad had come home from Germany. He had been in a labor-camp, digging man-holes on the side of roads. When he escaped, he walked during the night hours and hid during the day, in wet man-holes and gullies. He was very sick. He had large blisters on his feet, his shoes were completely worn out, and his feet had been frostbitten at times. Finding a doctor was not easy. Doctors were being watched and were questioned by the Germans. If they were to report my dad or other men who were hiding, these doctors would be in trouble, too. Eventually, and I don't know how, my mother found a doctor who was willing to come and see my dad. This was certainly an answer to her many prayers; she knew about the power of prayer. The doctor's diagnosis was that my dad had tuberculosis. Medication? I don't know. Eventually, on April 7, 1945 he passed away, just before we were liberated by the Allied Forces.

"Now everything changed again. For my mother, just making a living was a problem. She did get some help here and there.

Then she met a young woman who needed my mom's help. At the same time, this person was qualified to work with children, so a kind of children's home was started. Abandoned or neglected children were taken in and cared for. I became one of the group and. since I knew how things were done in the house, I had my work cut out for me, as young as I was.

"After a fight with my older brother, my mother took me apart and talked to me. Then and there, at the age of seven, I accepted the Lord. It was much later that the Lord began to open my heart to the possibility of serving Him. However, our doctor advised my mother and me against my becoming a nurse.

It was decided that I should pursue a teaching career: kindergarten and first and second grade.

I did get my certification for teaching and I enjoyed working with children, but my training involved a different approach to teaching, I was of the 'new school' and schools still preferred teachers who had been trained in the old way. That made it hard for a newly trained teacher to find a position.

"I met Fred in a Youth for Christ Camp in August 1958. I was the cook at that camp and he was a camper. I was from the north and he was a 'southerner'. A different accent!! But there in that camp, when I discovered that Fred was interested in going to the mission field, I realized that my desire to serve the Lord, which had started many years before, could become a reality. That is, if I could meet Fred's 'requirements'! He had three requirements for any prospective wife: being born again, being a nurse, and having black hair. I was born again, I was a teacher, rather than a nurse, and I had blond hair. Look at him now: what a compromiser! BUT: I did become an RN and studied midwifery, since I could not find a job in teaching. No black hair, though!

"In the beginning, my mother was against my dropping teaching and becoming a nurse. She had paid for all my education. However, as I showed my willingness to honor her wishes, the Lord began to work in her heart. The day came that she encouraged me to apply to a hospital to get my training. I was accepted after the first application, in spite of the fact that the course had started six weeks earlier. Here again we saw God's hand in our lives."

Fred: "Now it is my turn. After all, I was born five days later than Trudy. I was born in the south of the Netherlands, close to the borders with Germany and Belgium. I, too, was the youngest in the family, but the youngest of seven children. I had three older sisters and three older brothers.

"I was told that the first time I was in church was when I was just over one week old. I was not in a nursery, but in my mother's arms at first, and later on her lap. When I was a little older I began to sing the hymns and learned many of them by heart. The sermons were too long, but I could put my head on my mother's lap again. By the intonation of the pastor's voice I could tell when the sermon came to an end.

"Singing hymns while washing dishes with my sisters, we would sing in harmony, and I learned to sing the different parts of some of the hymns. Actually, I liked listening to Bible stories, too. I loved to hear about what Jesus did and said.

"After the war was over (November 1944) in the south of the Netherlands, my dad had to go on a business trip to Belgium and he brought back bananas. How all my siblings and my parents laughed when I asked, "How do I eat this thing?" I had never seen bananas before. Well, I was the youngest in the family: last one born, but the first one BORN AGAIN! A couple of years later, one of my sisters and her husband came to know the Lord. Just keep in mind: we were all extremely 'churchy'. Is that a word?

"It was during our second, but short, furlough in 1970 that, after I had a long talk with my mother, she too was blessed with assurance of salvation. That is what she wrote to us, when we were back in the jungle. She shared this verse with us in a letter:

Isaiah 49:15: 'Behold, I have graven thee upon the palms of My hands...!' What a blessing it was to receive this news from her!

"My dad became a believer many years later. The Lord had been speaking to him through Romans 3:23-24, but verse 24 had been impressed on his thinking for some time: "Being justified freely by His grace through the redemption that is in Christ Jesus." That had been his struggle, having been taught that nobody can 'know' for sure whether or not he has received the gift of salvation.

"On his birthday in 1986, I spent quite a bit of time with my dad. That morning nobody else was present yet. Trudy was two hours away. I had dropped her off to visit her mother, who had her birthday that same day. I was able to speak very openly to my dad. Both my parents had noticed the change in my life when, twenty and more years before, I had made a decision for the Lord and began to grow spiritually. It had always been easy to talk to my dad about theological things, but not about a daily personal walk with Him, nor about accepting His offer of salvation. In my home, the Bible was read at least once a day, after a meal, and we usually had three meals together as a family.

"A few months later, in 1986, I was able to speak to my dad one more time, by phone. He was in the hospital and would not go home again. My last question to him was: "Dad, do you remember the long talk we had on your birthday? How about that matter now?" His answer was: "Everything is in order now, my son!"

"When I found my mom's Bible in their home, later on, I noticed that my dad had been underlining verses in that Bible. That is something my mom would have never done. You see, although we were far away on the mission field for many years, and did not have the usual family times with our parents, now we know that there is an ETERNITY in which to have fellowship with them.

"A large Roman Catholic church was located across the street from our home, in which I lived during the first nine years of my life. The priest used to visit all the homes in his parish once a year. He knew that we were not Roman Catholic, but he may have thought that by visiting our family he would be able to proselytize. We were the only non-Roman-Catholics in that whole section of the city. The main reasons for visiting each home were: to encourage parents to be more faithful in attending the services; and to encourage parents to have more children. After all, when their youngest child is two years of age, the parents should be thinking about having their next baby. But the third reason was to encourage the parents to urge at least one of their sons and daughters to become a priest or a nun. When he began to notice that I was understanding what he was saying, he turned to me, and did that every year. He asked me if I would think about becoming a priest. "No!" was my response. "I am going to be a pastor!"

"Each afternoon I had to take a nap in those early years of my childhood, during WWII. Often I could not sleep and got up from my bed and held my own service – the kind I was familiar with in the church we attended. I used to stand up and sing one of the hymns, which I had learned in church and from my mother. Then I climbed up on top of a sturdy table, and "preached." Getting down from the table again, I would sing more hymns and then get back up again on the table and preach again. I never took up an offering, though!! I never heard whether or not my mother ever listened to these private and exclusive church services.

"Regularly there were funeral processions going from that Roman Catholic church to the cemetery around the corner. I followed the crowd at times, and somehow found my place right close to the grave. When the coffin was lowered into that hole, I could look down. Coming home, I asked my mother what was going to happen to the person inside that coffin. Where was he or she going? And she used to tell me that it was either heaven or hell, and I had heard about that already. "But what should I do to go to heaven?" I asked her. "Being a good boy will make you go to heaven!" But how good? I knew I had missed my chance already.

"Eventually, at the age of twelve, while in the public swimming pool with my best friend, I was offered the opportunity to receive an answer to my questions. He invited me to go to meetings for young people, in the fellowship hall of the church. There were two missionaries who had come to our church. One was from Canada, if I remember well, and one was from the United States, Henry Heijermans. With his knowledge of the Dutch language, he was the one who translated what was taught from English into Dutch. The invitation was clear, although I do not remember anything of the message. Henry dealt with me afterwards. I can still remember the spot in that fellowship hall. That was in August 1952.

"From that time on I attended the Bible studies for young people, led by Henry, in his home. We were always treated to American home-baked cookies, which his wife Cathy provided. It was about a six-mile walk every Wednesday. Later on, I went by bike. The next few years I went to summer camps, first in the south of the Netherlands and afterwards in the north. During a camp on the coast of the country, close to a beach, things became clearer to me about living for the Lord. During the campfire gathering, on a Friday night, we were all challenged about serving the Lord. After the fire had just about gone out, and only some ambers were left, the invitation was given: "Has the Lord spoken to anyone here about serving Him fulltime?" Yes, he had spoken to me.

Everybody had been asked to close their eyes. "What difference does that make?" I thought. And when I looked up I saw four hands go up. Not mine. I refused to raise my hand. But from that moment on, I knew that this was what the Lord wanted for my life, and that is what I wanted. Looking back, I am sorry to say that none of the other four young people ended up in the Lord's service. It reminds me of what Jesus said: "Son, go work today in my vineyard!" Matthew 21: 28-32, the parable of the two sons. One said "Yes," and did not go. The other said: "I will not!" and went. It is only by God's grace that He led me all the way!

"In the following years, I attended that kind of camp again, in a different location, but with the same emphasis. However, the camp in 1958 was completely different, because Trudy and I met and God's plan for our lives together became clear to both of us. We began to understand that God was knitting our hearts together. Right from that moment, we made it our practice always to pray together, whenever the Lord allowed us to be together. At that time, we lived about 150 miles from each other.

"Right then and there in that camp, things became difficult for Trudy. Her cooking was great, but one of the leaders criticized her about other things, including the fact that she and I were spending quite a bit of time together. We both remember how, at that time, we turned to John 15, about the fruit tree and the pruning. Pruning is what we needed at that time, and many times thereafter. A few months after leaving that camp, Trudy started her medical training. I went to England to become more fluent in English, so I could attend the European Bible Institute in France and take the classes in English. We will share more about this later."

"Train up a child in the way he should go..." Proverbs 22:6

Chapter 15

Our Family

We, as parents, had spent many, many hours in learning the Trio language. We were amazed at how quickly Rosyanne and Artwin learned it. FAST! At times they would say things to us about what they had been doing, but they could only tell us in the Trio language. We would ask, "What does that word mean?"

One of those times, they had been playing with other children on the rocks and in the river, in front of the village. We remember very well how Rosyanne was telling us, at lunch time, what she and other girls had been doing. I cannot even remember anymore the word she used, as we would never do that kind of thing, and I never used it in my Bible translation either. Something like: jumping in the water and making several cartwheels. No, Trudy did not do that either!

What fun our children had with each other and with the children in the village; Rosyanne with a couple of girls her age and Artwin with a bunch of boys his age. Artwin's best friend's name was Nowa. Trudy was 'hut-schooling' our children from about eight till eleven each morning. Their friends knew that, and stayed away. But once they were done, all of them went their different ways.

When it was time to eat, around one in the afternoon, we just had to use our special 'family whistle'. Several 'rascals' in the village could imitate it, and at times would use that whistle to get our attention. But if our whistle did not reach our children, to tell them to come home for lunch, others would repeat it. That helped!

One day, only Rosyanne came home and could not tell us where Artwin was, so we went out into the village square, in front of our house, and began asking the people we saw. We went farther and farther away from our house, until someone said that she had seen him with some other boys. So we went in the direction that she pointed out to us. No Artwin! No other boys either! We continued on until one of the women was able to tell us that Artwin and Nowa and two other boys had gone to the river and that they had a gun with them. Had Artwin taken my twelve-gauge Winchester? We quickly went home. Yes, the gun was gone, and some shells as well! How did he know which shells to take? I had three boxes, of different calibers, in that closet.

We quickly went to the river and got into our canoe, and started the outboard motor. After about fifteen minutes or so, we noticed a canoe under the branches of a tree, near the riverbank. That was at the beginning of a hunting trail. With the men who were with us, we quickly went looking for them. We walked a distance and listened; walked again and listened again. Then up a hill and just before we reached the top, we could hear the voices of the boys. Then we saw them! As soon as Artwin saw us, he said, "Look at what we shot!" And up went his hand with a pheasant in it. "How did you know what shells to take for my gun, Artwin?" I said. "Nowa knew!" was his response. Now he knew, too!

Arriving back in the village, we were immediately told to go and see Tamenta, the wise and natural tribal leader. The four boys were told to sit down. "Do you realize what you did, you little ones?" Tamenta asked. "If anything had happened to you, the leaders in the city would have told us that we cannot buy shotgun shells anymore!" Then he sent us home with Artwin; he talked to Nowa and the other two boys.

The food was cold now. But we were thankful that all had gone well and that the Lord had protected the boys! We could still thank God for the food and for His protection. On one occasion earlier, the Lord had not protected Artwin.

We had built a water tower with posts from the jungle — the kind that won't rot 'before your great-grand-children are born', as the Trios told us. It was about forty feet high, and held six fifty-five gallon drums of water on the top. At the bottom were also nine of those drums. From time to time we pumped up the rainwater, which we caught from the metal roof of the clinic. We used that water during the rainy season, when the rivers flushed all the debris from the creeks. We had running water in our house and in the clinic, and there were two more spots in the village where people could get their own drinking water.

I was working on top of the tower and needed electricity for what I was doing. For that reason I had started the diesel generator. Normally we used it only at night for lights in our house, the church, and in a number of Indian huts. Because of the noise, I had buried a fifty-five gallon drum in the ground, behind that generator shed. A pipe went from the shed into the drum, so that the engine would not make too much noise – an improvised 'muffler'. While working, several boys were playing close to the shed, and Artwin must have decided that the pipe was at a nice height to hang from or swing on. Then I heard a loud scream from Artwin, followed by screams from the other boys. I do not remember how I came down from that tower and reached Artwin, some forty or fifty yards away. Quickly we went to the clinic, where Trudy was working. Ointment could take care of the wounds, but not the pain and tears. Eventually Trudy gave him a shot of something, which put him to sleep. He slept well until the next morning!

Children in the village did not have toys from the outside world. They made their own toys, like wooden airplanes, complete with little propellers, made from old pieces of roofing. Rosyanne and Artwin had homemade toys, too, but we had also bought two scooters for our children. At times they looked like 'flying Dutchmen', as they raced through the village, in between the huts and on the airstrip. On one of our walks through the village, we noticed some boys on those scooters, but as soon as they saw us coming, they dropped the scooters in high grass and they themselves disappeared into the cassava fields. We did not see them come out again but, later that afternoon, we noticed the same boys playing in the village. We assured them that it was all right for them to ride those scooters, as long as our children gave them permission. They looked so relieved! But why should we tell you everything?

Maybe, rather than telling the stories for them, we should let our children share some of their experiences.

Rosyanne:

"We were walking through the village one day, stopping to talk with people here and there. I am not sure what it was that made me look at Duchesse, our Dalmatian dog, and decide that I wanted to pretend that she was my 'horse'. I climbed up on her back and held on as much as I could. She didn't like it! She took off running with me on her back. Not being able to hold on to her, I fell off after about ten to fifteen yards, scraping my elbows and knees. I never tried this trick again!"

"How did I come to know the Lord? We had our daily devotions as a family, and we joined the Indian children in their special meetings every Wednesday afternoon. We heard so much about the Lord and accepting the Lord. I must have been about seven years old and had done something that required me to be 'set back on track'. I had been told to go to my room. This was always a good approach as it allowed me time to think; it also allowed my parents time to gain calmness and perspective before coming back to talk with me. Somehow, this time, I lay on my bed, feeling a real sense of having been wrong, having sinned. In my mind, someone who had sinned, and didn't set things right with God, was going to end up in hell. I would not be going to heaven then, and wouldn't be together with my parents. How terrible!

"So, in my young, limited but profound, understanding of everything, I realized I needed to set things right with God. I cannot really remember which of my parents ended up coming into my little room, to talk about what I had done. But, once we had talked through the situation, we talked about disobedience and sin and I asked Jesus into my heart." *[It was Trudy who joined her first, but then called me]*

Now it is **Artwin's** turn:

"All I remember is that we were in Langhorne, Pennsylvania, at the mission headquarters. We had been traveling, visiting churches, and raising support. Whenever we were not on the road, we stayed in the basement apartment of the mission's headquarters. I felt that I should accept Christ, which I did. I had been to all the missionary meetings, the youth activities in the church we attended and heard so much of the Bible. I was also present when meetings with the young people in Tepoe were held. I believe all four of us were there. Our brother Vincent was not born yet, as he was added to our family later. We became quite an international bunch of kids: Rosyanne was born in the Netherlands, I was born in Suriname, and Vincent in Luxembourg.

"As I was really young, just seven years of age, I do not remember the exact reason why I felt the need to accept Christ that day. That was the beginning of my life as a Christian. As children, we had seen our dad baptize quite a number of people, after leaving Suriname in 1972.

"Finally it was time for Rosyanne and me to take that step of obedience. Our parents never put pressure on us; they talked about it but left that decision up to us. When we were ready to take that step, it was decided that we would be baptized in the village and among the people we grew up with, PËRËRU TEPOE...TOAD ROCK, where we had experienced so much and where we had seen many Indians being baptized in the river. That opportunity presented itself in 1981, when as a family of five, we had the joy of spending six weeks in the village in which we had lived during the first years of our lives. So our baptism was in the Tapanahony River!"

As parents, Trudy and I talked to the church leaders in Tepoe. They were excited about our being there and now the possibility of baptizing 'their teacher's children'. Both Rosyanne and Artwin would have to give their testimonies of how they accepted the Lord, and also to share some of their inward spiritual struggles as children and young people.

How amazed these Indians were that our children had experiences in their daily spiritual lives that were similar to those of their own children. After the morning service we went to the river, to a spot close to the house where we had lived in for many years, and were living in then again!

Then, with the whole village present, I had the privilege of baptizing both Rosyanne and Artwin, together with Pisere, the leading pastor in the village.

We had dedicated Rosyanne in our own room in the Netherlands, together with some friends, before leaving for Suriname. Artwin was dedicated in an English-speaking congregation in Paramaribo, which was led by the missionary pilot Roy Parsons. Vincent was dedicated in the French-speaking church in Luxembourg. Later on, as father, I had the privilege of baptizing Vincent in Maastricht, in the Netherlands.

Although Vincent was not part of our family yet, when we lived in Tepoe, he had a number of opportunities to be with us there, later. Those were the times when we were able to go back for six weeks of Bible teaching, once a year, which temporarily came to an end in the spring of 1986.

"MY WORD...shall not return unto ME void...."

Chapter 16

The Inter-Tribal Bible School

When we were in the village of Tepoe in 1993 for the first Inter-Tribal Bible School, we noticed five young Indians in the front row. They were diligently writing down the notes that we put on the blackboard; actually, the board was green. When we asked some of the Trios who they were, their response was: "They are Apalais from Brazil, and they came with Warema and his family!" Warema is a Trio who is married to a Wayana. The whole family had fled to Brazil during the interior fighting, which started shortly after we had left Tepoe in early 1986.

At the end of the one-month teaching period, one of these young men came to see me, and showed me the notes he had taken during that month. Then he proceeded to tell me that he was going to take these notes, and teach his father, who happened to be the Chief of the Apalai Indians. We were told that, about two years later, this father accepted the Lord as well. So many of the people we are telling you about are already with the Lord. They beat us to it!! This includes this chief.

But right away, the young man and his friends began to ask if we could come and conduct a similar Bible School for their own people in his village in Brazil. What a wonderful invitation, but not something that would be feasible. The officials across the border were not open to missionaries coming to that part of the country. Unfortunately, we had to share that information with them. When these five and many more returned to Tepoe the next year, they renewed their request. But now the Trios and Wayanas, who were doing missionary work in their area, joined the Apalais in their request. Again we had to give them the same answer. Some more people came from Brazil in 1995, to attend the one-month teaching period. They did have copies of the New Testament, translated for them by a Wycliffe couple from the United States, but they did not have the books of the Old Testament. They do now!

The Trios did have portions of the Old Testament, as we had started translating them in 1993.

Some books, which they had already, we could revise. When all these men continued insisting on having us teach the Bible in their main village, we got the idea of having these Bible-teaching months closer to the border with Brazil, but still in Suriname.

"That is what we have been thinking about ourselves!" was their answer. Now the ball was in their court! At the end of the month, a whole group of men and women wanted to talk to us again. They were willing to clear an area in the south of Suriname, close to the border with Brazil. They would pick the place and do all the work. "We want to do that near the end of the year, December 1995, or in January. But will you come and join us when we go?" they asked. "Well, yes, if this is what the Lord wants. We all need to pray about it and the Lord needs to provide the funds for us to return at that time!" we replied.

They made plans, and we started praying about it. Our decision was that the Lord would have to provide the funds for the plane tickets, the flight to the village of Tepoe or Paloemeu, the funds for the river trip, and everything else that would be needed. We prayed and prayed, but by the end of November that year, not one penny had been donated toward this project! So now we had to disappoint our Indian brothers and sisters in the Lord again. No Bible School sessions in their area, and no starting a new camp for Bible teaching in Suriname either. Soon afterwards we discovered the reasons why the Lord had not allowed us to be part of these activities.

Just before Christmas that year, lightning had struck in the village of Tepoe and traveled from one side of a hut to the other side, during a heavy tropical rainstorm. A number of the women had been thrown to the ground and one of them was killed by the lightning strike. She was the wife of one of the Trio men who would have been involved in looking for a place to build the new camp, and to start cutting trees in that area.

A second reason why the Lord stopped us from going on that trip, we discovered less than one year later. In August 1996, as we flew to Tepoe for the annual Bible School period, we noticed a canoe on the river, traveling toward the Brazil border. It was loaded with a group of men and lots of gear. They had decided to tackle the project themselves: looking for a good place, and beginning to cut an area for a building and their own huts. They missed the Bible teaching, but started a project and a ministry that was going to be a blessing to many Indians from several tribes. All this activity did not go unnoticed by people from the outside. Soon we found out that people in the city were saying that Trios had been cutting 'Fred's Camp' in the south of Suriname. God had spared us from another 'attack' on the Lord's work. "No," the Indians said, "this is our camp, and not Fred's!"

However, now we had the privilege of helping Trios, Wayanas and Akuriyos in fulfilling their vision of reaching more people with the Gospel, and receiving more teaching from the Word. In October 1996, after the Bible School period in Tepoe, we traveled down the Tapanahony River and up the Paloemeu River. It was a trip that took four days, using four large canoes, with a total of fifty-four people in it: fifty Indians; two Mission Aviation men from the coast, Rick and Richard; a hard-working fellow from Iowa, Ryan; and myself.

As soon as the two canoes arrived at the clearing in the jungle, some men started burning what had been cut two months before.

In the month that followed, the first six-hundred-foot length and over sixty-foot-width of the cut area was completely cleared of tree stumps and limbs. Sometimes the women had to dig down four feet or more to get some of the stumps and roots out. This was done while we men were cutting limbs with axes and two chainsaws, but then we needed to roll everything off to the side to be burned. All the expenses were covered by one of our supporting churches in Strawberry Point, Iowa. The heat from the sun and the burning wood brought the temperature up to close to one hundred forty degrees, at times. Some of the women constantly brought all the workers all kinds of beverages to drink, as our skins looked like 'porous cloth'. In between, the men had been working hard to enlarge the length of the cleared area from six hundred feet to fifteen hundred feet. That is the minimum length civil aviation specified for an airstrip. It was a tremendous job, and we always started the day with devotions and singing and praying.

All fifty-four of us stayed on an island across the river, as the ashes made it impossible to sleep where all the work took place. But this happy and blessed month of hard work had to come to an end.

We ran out of food and fuel. As with all our time with the Indians, whether it was the years we lived with them in a village, or the months and months we spent with them, during the years thereafter, when we had left them 'officially' and ministered in Europe, these were times of spiritual enrichment for ourselves. Living so close to them in a camp, and living the way they did, made us feel like part of their families and lives. They often said that we were part of them:

"You look like us, with your suntan, and you act like us, and you speak our language!" they often said.

But the work was not done yet! We needed to go back to Kënepaku, named after the rapids right at the camp. That happened in early 1997. Simple huts were built on the side of the river, in the area that had been cleared several months before. It was the official rainy season, but the real rains did not come until the end of our stay. On our way back to Paloemeu, the first tropical rainstorm accompanied us for about four hours, complete with thunder and lightning. It is not a good thing to hide under the trees!

More stumps had to be removed, material had to be brought in from the surrounding area to construct the building where the Bible teaching would take place. One hundred fifty-five six-foot galvanized sheets of roofing were flown to the Paloemeu airstrip downriver. These, too, had to come up to the camp, the same way we had come: one day up the river, then over a trail, up a hill, bypassing the five or six waterfalls, called 'Turn-back Falls'. Then all of it was loaded into different canoes again, followed by another more than one-hour trip up the river. Then there was a trek through the jungle for ninety minutes or more. How thankful we have always been that the Lord spared all of us from harm and disease! Lots of huts were built.

During the summer of 1997 we held the first Inter-tribal Bible School sessions in this new camp. Indians came from different tribes and different villages in Suriname. We spent afternoons in finishing the building of the airstrip, which was opened in early 1998. Also, Indians from Brazil and French Guyana attended, and the outreach of the Trio churches increased. About one hundred fifty eager students, representing five different tribes, were present for that first Bible School period. One year we had more than two hundred fifty people in attendance. As I taught in Trio, Warema translated into Wayana. Sometimes we were interrupted when someone from a different tribe did not completely understand what we were saying. Notebooks, ballpoint pens, highlighters, and newly translated portions of the Old Testament were distributed during the first Sunday of each month.

During this time, we experienced the way in which many of the men learned to teach the Word of God to people in their villages, and in their tribes. Each morning two men were appointed by some of the church leaders, to teach for about twenty minutes a portion of what they had learned in the morning. Yes, some knees were knocking behind that big pulpit, and we also saw trembling hands, and sweat coming down from some faces. But many of them who came back a year later were rejoicing in the fact that the Lord was using them, in a different way than before, in their own villages and tribes. We rejoiced in hearing from them!

One of the Wayana men, together with his wife, came to see us in our hut. "Father!" he said, "I have been a song leader in my church for over twenty years. Now I want to start teaching God's Paper, too!" In short, I told him that he should go and talk to those who were in charge of the Bible School, and let them know. He did! Then the day came that his name appeared on the board, to teach that evening. As all the other men did every day, in the afternoon, he came over to our hut to share what he wanted to teach that evening. As soon as I asked him some questions about the passage and chapter he had chosen, he began to sweat profusely. He had a hard time answering questions, but also in asking questions. After about one hour he and his wife left again, with my encouragement to pray and read his own notes, together with his wife.

"I don't know what it is going to be like tonight!" I said to Trudy after he left. That evening the man got up and as soon as he took his place behind the pulpit, we could see his forehead dripping already. It was a difficult beginning. But once he really got started, the words started flowing. After about twenty minutes, he said: "If I do not quit now, I will still be teaching tomorrow morning!"

As with all the other men, when they were finished teaching, I got up and critiqued him, to help improve his teaching; this allowed everyone to hear my comments and learn as well. Two weeks later, the same man had another chance to teach, and everybody was astonished at how well he did. The following year he came back and right away shared with us that he had become one of the teachers in the church. And then he hastened to add: "I brought my son this year, the one who leads the singing now in the church; he lost his wife last November. I want him to start teaching, too!"

We explained that it could be done in the same way as for him. They needed to talk to the leaders, which they did that day. Soon his son's name appeared on the board and one afternoon he showed up with his New Testament and notes. "What do you want to teach the people tonight?" I asked.

"I want to talk about the passage in 1 Thessalonians 4, the one you taught the other day!" I was amazed that he had chosen that passage about the return of the Lord, and the dead in Christ being raised. "You know," I said, "you will be able to teach that better than I can! I have not lost my wife. That is an experience I have not had. I know what it teaches, but that experience of death I have not had!"

That evening he went through those verses one by one, and then started sharing his experience of losing his wife, and what he was looking forward to. All those in attendance listened attentively. You must know that the Bible School building has a dirt floor but, as the saying goes, 'You could have heard a pin drop!'

Let us go back to something else that happened before the first group of Trios left Tepoe, to start building the camp. After teaching one morning in the church at Tepoe, one of the younger men came to see us in our house, which had the same structure as an Indian hut: thatched roof, all jungle material in the roof and walls, but off the ground.

It was Muta, whom we had known from the years we lived with the Indians in their village from 1965 till 1972. He was probably one or two years older than our own children. We knew his parents and his grandparents, all of whom had become believers when we lived with them in the 1960's and 1970's. We were there for their baptisms.

This is what he came to share with us: "I received Jesus many years ago, when you lived in our village, but I have not lived for God. When listening to your teaching from God's Paper, I decided that I now want to be baptized and live for God!" Well, the conversation was a little longer than that.

"I am so glad to hear that," was my response. "It makes me rejoice! But you must tell the elders of the church. You know that we are only here to teach you God's Paper. We are not leaders in the church or village!"

His response was: "I know, but I wanted you to know it first.

When I leave your 'hut', I am going to meet with the church leaders. I will tell them what I just told you!"

Checking with some of these church leaders later that day, we found out that Muta had indeed shared his thoughts with them. "What are you going to do about it?" I asked. "We are going to baptize him, because he is ready for it!" While we were still present, we saw Muta go into the river, the waters of baptism, and everybody heard his testimony.

All of this happened about a year before the idea of building a camp for a Bible School was brought up. As soon as this project started being discussed, Muta came back to our house. Now he wanted to share with us that he wanted to be involved in building the camp. Again, we had to tell Muta that this too had to be discussed with the church leaders, rather than with us. He agreed!

After he left, it did not take long for another Trio, about the same age as Muta, to come and talk to us. He wanted to share his thoughts and desires with us as well. "I have taught the children in school for more than twenty-two years, but now I want to serve the Lord!" he said. I could have explained to Sinëkë that he had served the Lord in that school all those years, but if he felt as though he needed to change, he should make that decision before the Lord. Wow! What was the Lord doing? Both of these men were 'jewels,' who eventually would play an extremely important role in the Bible School Camp ministry in the following twenty-one years.

Muta was completely in charge of all the logistics of each Bible School period. He knew how many temporary huts were needed every year, as well as how many canoes were needed to transport everyone from the Brazilian border to the camp, and from Paloemeu to Kënepaku. He organized the cutting of the new gardens, so there would be enough food for the hundreds of Indians in attendance, the following year. He was in charge of making new forty-five-foot canoes. And he informed me if extra lights and wiring were needed, as well as how much fuel would be needed and sometimes parts for outboard motors. He wrote all this in a letter, the pilot and his staff scanned the letter, and the request reached us by email here in the USA. After we okayed the purchase of these things, the pilot and his crew did the buying for us before we arrived in Suriname. Muta also organized the radio contacts every day during the Bible School. The short-wave radio was under the roof of our hut, on the outside.

Sinëkë had a completely different ministry at the camp. He organized all the meetings: which tribe would start the session with singing, who would lead in prayer at the beginning, and which people were going to be prayed for, from other villages and tribes, especially those who were sick or in a hospital. That kind of information was collected by short-wave radio, even from villages in Brazil. On Sundays, he put together the whole order of service. On those days every tribe had its own singing group and each tribe could sing three songs. Since there were usually five tribes represented every year, the song service often lasted about two hours. For that reason, the leaders decided that each tribe could sing only one song. That did not sit well with most of the singers. As a result, each tribe sang one song three times. Singing is such a vital part of all services for these dear people!

Muta and Sinëkë made life so easy for us. We were just told what to do every day. Sinëkë would also inform me when the church leaders of the different villages and tribes wanted to talk to me. Many afternoons they all met to discuss church situations in the different villages. "Just call me when you are ready for me!" was always my answer. At times he did, but other days he did not. And when I asked him before the evening service why he had not called me, he answered: "We did not need you! Together we came to a conclusion and decided what to do in problem cases, in a particular tribe or village!" That is the way we wanted them to be, learning to rely on God for guidance.

The last evening of each Bible School month, we had a testimony service. Nobody needed to be prodded to participate. It proceeded in a very orderly fashion, as Sinëkë told them that we would sing a song, and then three of them could come forward and share. At the end of the song, different ones got up and the three who got to the pulpit first gave their testimony. Then another song, and further sharing; that was repeated for the rest of the evening, starting at seven o'clock till somewhere between ten and eleven.

The following morning, Monday, everybody left the camp, rejoicing and well-fed spiritually.

Here, in brief, is what they shared with all in attendance after the month when the book of Ezekiel was taught:

"Ezekiel 28 tells us about Satan's pride and I can see pride in my own life as well!"

"Ezekiel 34:11 tells me that the Lord will take care of the sheep. That is what we should be doing, as leaders in our churches. If I allow evil things in my life, it will get worse. Only if I stay in the WORD I can overcome."

"Ezekiel 8:12: The people said that God does not see in the dark. Therefore, God left them. I too can continue to sin, but that means that I am laughing at God!"

"Ezekiel 24 tells us about Jerusalem being a boiling pot. I would be very unhappy to hear something like that being said about my village."

"Ezekiel 8 speaks about idol worship. Whatever my idols are, they bring dishonor to His name. Then I destroy His temple. Having learned this here, I say 'thank you' to God and to my teacher!"

"In Ezekiel 34:10 God says that He does not like those shepherds and that He Himself will take care of the sheep. These are warnings for us who are teachers in our villages!"

Each year, during the Bible School, various different subjects, Bible books, and passages were taught:

Ps 1:1 Blessed is the man who does NOT: walk...stand...sit....
"This really stung me. It hurt me inside when I heard it. Isn't this what we do, when we go to a village where they have fermented drink? We walk in slowly, and get closer and closer. Then we stand at a distance and get even closer to watch them. Then we sit down and become one of them!"

"The Messiah is King! Do I really let HIM be my King?"

"1 Tim 6:15 It made me rejoice! At the same time: How will I meet HIM?"

Rev. 19:16 "He is: The King of kings, the Lord of Lords!"

Ps 45:12-17 & Eph 5:27 "He gave Himself for us, His church and is holy. I have failed in these things."

Psalm 1:3 "That is what I desire to be! A tree planted by the rivers of water, bringing forth fruit!"

"In the Messianic Psalms, He shows Himself as God and Creator.
He will show Himself KING. Romans 14:11 ALL will bend their knees."

Psalm 1:4 ...like chaff!! "Am I that way?"

2 Corinthians 5:10: "We must all appear before the judgment seat of Christ: faithful children of God... and pretenders...."

"Psalm 1 made me happy and sad! I am at times like both of these two."

"Blood of sheep speaks about God's wrath. Heb 12:24 tells us why HE died. In the OT blood was shed to cover sin. In the NT blood was shed to wash away our sin. HE died to do this for me! There was NO ONE like HIM before! Paul asked: Why do we still sin?

"HE DIED, HE ROSE and I arose too. Jesus was faithful when tested by people for three years. I may be faithful for 2 days!"

"Psalm 1 hurt me! How can I be? How are we at times?
It made me ashamed!"

"What father taught us hurt me! Psalm 1 made me ashamed.
It hit me hard!"

"We know that Adam hurt God. And Jesus was also hurt by people! At times we do the same with our lives. Let us remember
2 Corinthians 5:21: HE knew no sin, but was made sin for us. We receive God's righteousness through HIM!"

Psalm 120:1 "I cried for help and HE heard it. These words I heard with JOY! Obey and there will be blessing. Disobey and there will be hardship."

2 Tim 3:16 "All of the Word is inspired by God's Spirit:
doctrine, reproof, correction, instruction. Do we want to be happy or ashamed?"

Each year it was such a joy for us to notice what the Lord was doing, as He used His Word in the lives of these men and women. For the boys and girls, we had Vacation Bible School for many years.

We started each Bible School on a Sunday and ended on a Sunday. There were plenty of occasions to share the Gospel with those attending, although these times were supposed to be mainly for training the current and potential church leaders. However, there would always be some in attendance who had never made a decision for Jesus Christ. So usually on the fourth Sunday we gave an invitation for salvation or rededication. At times there were between ten and twenty who raised their hands and later, at the end of the service, they came forward.

Then I turned the service over to the elders and deacons. They knew their own people and could deal with them individually. When some came to confess their sinful walk, these men could minister to them. They knew them. They knew what had happened in their villages, and were better qualified than I was to counsel with them. It was often difficult for me to really understand what had happened in their lives, and what the situation was in their local churches.

After everyone had left one year, we were a bit disappointed that we had seen no salvations that year.

We were encouraged, though, by the testimonies we had heard, showing us that the Spirit had been at work.

There was more work to do on translation, so a group of men stayed behind to check out the documents which we had brought. Some men had taken Indians back to the Brazil border, to return home. Muta and others had gone downriver to the Paloemeu airstrip to drop off folks there, to return to their villages. A few days later the canoes came back and we noticed a fellow whom we had not seen for many years.

That afternoon, from our hut we could see that some men were talking together in the Bible School building. When I approached them, I also saw the visitor who had come back with the canoes. So now I could greet him! After I sat down and listened to them talking, the first ones got up and left the building. Slowly they all left, one by one, and I was left alone with this young man. I started talking to him, but realized that he did not speak the Trio language all that well. (His first language was Wayana.) But we could understand each other. I directed the conversation toward the Lord and salvation. Then he said: "I wanted to be here at the Bible School this year, but my boss wanted me to take tourists on their hike through the jungle!"

In further questioning him, it became clear to me that he was not a believer, but at the same time it was obvious that he was very open to the Gospel, or maybe I should say that he was ready to accept the Lord. My hesitation was that maybe my talk with him was not completely understood, so I asked him if he wanted to talk to one of the believers and speak in his own language. He accepted that idea right away. Fortunately, there was someone in the camp, who was also helping me with translation, who spoke the Wayana language fluently, although he was a Trio. So we went together to the other side of the camp, and I shared the information with this man, a church leader from the village of Paloemeu, the same village this young man was from. After explaining the situation to him, I left them to be by themselves. Later that evening we were told that this man had accepted the Lord. What a victory! That made that one-month Bible School even more precious to us.

Although we never kept records of all those who attended these Bible School periods, we estimate that between three and four thousand Indians from several different tribes attended.

Of course, many of them came every year, or almost every year.

Others came several times, and some just once or twice.

The cost of these times of teaching in the Bible School went up to fifteen thousand dollars per year. Every year those funds came in, in different ways, and from different sources. One year, someone contacted our mission, asking about funds for the Bible School. "How much is needed?" was his question. "Six thousand dollars is still needed!" was the answer he received. "Shall I send that by money-order or check?" he asked. Our God is: Jehovah-Jireh!

What a blessing it was when the first five Apalais attended the Bible School for the first time in 1993! At that time we had no idea what was going to happen.

Once we started the teaching at Kënepaku, we saw many come from Brazil. In the beginning, they brought us a letter from the officials in Brazil with names; what village each person was from; date of departure; date of the Bible School, beginning and end; and the date when these people were expected back in Brazil. At one point, there was no letter. We asked them why there was no letter. "We don't need it, because they trust you!" Just think, this happened at a time when missionaries were not allowed to work in northern Brazil.

Then one year, one of the Trios came to talk to me. His father calls me 'yako', which means 'brother'. For that reason, this young fellow calls me 'father'. His question was: "Father, do you want to go to the Apalai village, to teach there?" I realized again that my answer would disappoint him, and probably others. "NO, I cannot go, because the officials don't allow missionaries there!" This young man asked me the same question three times, as if he wasn't hearing what I told him each time.

Finally, he asked me: "Father, are you willing to go?" It was like he hit me on the head. "Oh, yes, I am willing!" I replied. "That is all the Apalais want to know!" he answered.

We talked a little more and prayed together. Then he left. Soon we found out that one of the Apalais in attendance was the son of a tribal leader in his village. He went to the short-wave radio by our hut and talked to his father. Then we heard that his father went by plane to the nearest large city to talk to the officials, asking permission for Trudy and me to visit, and to hold a Bible Conference in their main village.

As we arrived by canoe back in Paloemeu, planning to return to Paramaribo and then to fly on to Miami, another Indian approached us. He was an Apalai, too. "I will take your belongings to the plane!" he said. And while we walked together, he said: "So you are going to my village in Brazil!" "We may go, if the officials in your country give their permission!" I responded. "Oh, the papers are signed already!" he responded. That news had reached them already by radio from Brazil.

A few months later, Trudy and I were on our way to southern Brazil, and then we went from there to the east and then to the north. At the airport in Macapa, we were met by two Apalais. They were our interpreters. Just think, we speak six languages, but people from the jungle had to interpret for us into Portuguese.

They dropped us off at a pastor's home, where we spent the night.

Going . . . ! A Sacrifice?

The next morning, our Indian interpreters picked us up again and took us by taxi to the officials, who needed to record our presence and departure to the Apalai village. The Apalais had asked us when we were in Kënepaku if we would be able to bring some money for the flight to their village. Now they asked us if we had been able to bring some money. "Yes! We have four hundred American dollars!" we said. They were delighted. "But how much is the cost for the flight?" we asked. "That is twenty-four hundred!" they responded. "But we have the rest of the money, because of selling Indian curios in this city! When do you want to fly to our village? Today or tomorrow?"

"There is nothing we want to do in this city," we responded. "But is there a flight today?" we asked. "Yes, there is a flight. Let us go!" Off we went, back to the airport, and then on to the Apalai village, about two hours by plane.

What a reception by these people, of whom we had met so many already! Many met us on the airstrip, still wet from taking a bath. They had been working in their gardens, and had not expected the plane to come in that early. And now we finally met the father of the young man who had approached us in 1993, asking if we could come and teach in his village, where his father was the chief. A large group of Trios and Wayanas had traveled by canoe and then crossed the mountains between Suriname and Brazil. Apalais picked them up in the foothills and brought them to their village, by canoe.

What a time we had! We taught many hours each morning and then had other meetings the rest of the day. When I gave an invitation for those who wanted to receive the Lord, quite a large group of young people and children came forward and, in addition, several somewhat older Indians. One of them stood out to us. He was in his thirties, I think. Of course, we did not know who they were, but the church leaders took over from me. Later that week there was a baptismal service. This young man was among the ones being baptized. But as in Suriname, people who were going to be baptized had to give their public testimony first! As I was taking a video of the baptisms, Trudy stood close to Sinëkë and his wife Pekki. The young man's testimony was in Apalai, and therefore this dear couple translated for her. This is the most important part of what he said: "Not clubbed to death, but my heart pierced!"

Now you need to know the background to understand what this meant. We did not know the full story at that time, but when several weeks later we visited the couple who had translated the New Testament for that tribe, the Koehns, we heard the rest of the story.

This young man's mother had a hard time delivering him. Some Indians came to let these missionaries know that the mother could not deliver her baby. So they went to the village, where the mother was. As they climbed up the riverbank in that village, they heard the baby crying. The baby was born! But when they went to the hut, where the delivery had just taken place, they found the mother in her hammock, and the baby on the ground. The missionary's wife cleaned up the baby as well as she could, and she tried to give the boy to his mother, but there was no reaction from inside the mosquito netting. Eventually she pulled up the mosquito netting, and gave the baby to the mother. At that time she and her husband did not know the custom in that culture: After birth, a baby must be picked up by the father. He is the only one who is allowed to do that. That constitutes the father's agreement that the baby should live. So actually, the baby's life was saved because of a lack of knowledge of the culture on the part of the missionaries.

But now this missionary couple found the term for the Biblical thought and word for salvation: 'lifted' or 'picked up'. That is exactly the word the Trios use as well: He is my 'lifter' or 'picker-upper'. You see: THE FATHER is the only ONE who can save! HE has done that by becoming 'MAN' in Jesus Christ. Next time you sing the chorus of that hymn: "Love lifted me," maybe you will want to sing, as Trudy and I always do: CHRIST LIFTED ME!

As this young man gave his testimony about salvation, he was referring to the fact that his father could have used a club to kill him. But he testified that the WORD of GOD, had pierced his heart. We have no idea as to exactly what it was during the teaching that pierced his heart. Not important, is it? THE WORD of GOD did it. As in all these cases, when people came to a personal knowledge of Jesus Christ, it was the WORD of GOD that did it! We were only the tools, which the Lord used.

"The Word of God is powerful and sharper than any two-edged sword, piercing even to the dividing asunder of soul and spirit...."

Hebrews 4:12.

And isn't there God's promise as well? "So shall My Word be that goeth forth out of My mouth: it shall not return unto Me void, but it shall accomplish that which I please, and it shall prosper in the thing whereto I sent it!" Isaiah 55:11.

Can you imagine the joy in the hearts of the Koehns when I handed them a letter from this young man? He had given it to us before we left their village. We did not know the contents of that letter. Trudy and I had no idea what God had been doing during that week. Yes, a number of people had responded to the invitation, and came forward. Yes, a number of people were baptized during that week, but when we visited the Koehns in Tennessee, the whole story was complete. They showed us an article which they had just written, telling about this incident at the time of the boy's birth. They wrote the beginning of the story, but when we gave them that letter, they received the last chapter of the story.

As we looked back over those years of ministry among these Indians, we realized that, while we knew that between three and four thousand Indians attended these annual Bible School sessions, we did not know the full impact on the participants. What has God done with these lives, and how has God used them in the furtherance of the Gospel?

"I am made all things to all men,
that I might by all means save some!" 1 Cor. 9:22b

Chapter 17

Cultural Things

As we write about these matters, we are well aware that many things have changed over the years. They do in every culture, and we experienced that when we returned to the Netherlands, after having been away for more than twenty-eight years. Even the way people express themselves is different. We heard words and expressions, when we arrived back in our 'native' country, that we never used when we were children. Our parents would have said, if we had used these words: "Go and wash your mouth out with soap!" That was enough for us to realize that that kind of language was not acceptable. Even in the Indian culture we have noticed many changes. But what we are about to share with you now are things we encountered while in Suriname, and especially among the Indians.

Even when we were in Paramaribo, in the early months of 1964, there were things we had to learn fast. We kept our eyes and ears open. Just as we had learned from this anthropologist while in linguistics training: "The people you go to are not different. You missionaries are different!" How different were we?

<u>Head covering</u>

As we tried to learn our way about in the city, we put our daughter Rosyanne in a small stroller and walked all over the place. We got to know our way around and learned about the different stores. But we noticed how many Suriname ladies, wearing their folkloristic outfits, in those days, were looking at us and especially at Rosyanne, our then-four-month-old little girl. Our first thought was: she is so blond and so light-skinned and therefore they like her. But before too long, one of these women stopped us and told us that it was absolutely wrong to have our little girl outside without something on her head. "The head needs to be covered while out in the sun. And do not ever let her head get wet in the rain!" she told us. Such cruel white parents!! We quickly learned!

Easter

In some countries women wear white dresses for the Easter celebration. Even the week before Easter many of them used to wear white dresses. Trudy had no white dress. So we went to a store and we bought the material for a white dress. Trudy has always loved to sew; her father was a tailor, you remember, and she must have 'inherited' this skill from him. But when Easter Sunday arrived, Trudy was the only one who wore a white dress. Most women wore colorful clothing. Only during the "Passion Week" did the women wear white. We quickly learned!

Bonding with nationals

There is a good book on this subject. It speaks about missionaries learning about the new culture they have come to live in. It explains the mistakes that can be made, when new missionaries get all the information about that culture from other missionaries who have lived in that country for a long time already. It is called 'Orientation to the field' in some cases. Very often things can be 'interpreted' from the standpoint of the culture which missionaries have left behind.

Of course, there are things new missionaries can be warned about, but the best way to learn a new culture is by having open ears, open eyes, and open minds, and asking questions. Most people are pleased to hear 'foreigners' ask questions about their culture. Remember what we shared before, when an anthropologist warned us that 'we' as missionaries are different, and not the people we go to? Get it from the horse's mouth!

Right from the start, living in Ricanau Moffo, we had people around us all day. The men wanted to help me, and a number of the women wanted to help Trudy, especially holding our daughter Rosyanne. As I worked with these men, at times I would request assistance something like this: "Would you PLEASE do this for me, or get that for me?" After a day or two when I asked Simon to do something for me, he walked over to me and said: "Pastor, do not ask us to do that for you. Tell us what to do. If you ask us, as you are doing, we might say, NO!" Well that was hard. Of course, these people's ancestors had been brought from Africa to be slaves in Suriname. The first ones who came were used to being commanded. This had become part of their culture. To be honest, I never got used to ordering people about like that.

Later, when living with the Trios, we were faced with something similar. The Trio language also has an imperative form of verbs. I had the same feeling about commanding them, but there was a way around it with the Trios. You could say something like: "This needs to be done is....!" And right away that person, or more than one, would start doing it.

We learned those lessons as well, but sometimes the hard way. Early in our years among the Trios, actually it was within our first year, about five men offered to build a forty-five-foot canoe for us. One of the men came to borrow an axe from us. When eventually the canoe was built, we asked him about the axe. Well, he needed it to do something for himself. No problem! Much later, we asked him again, and we got the same response. Time after time, he refused to bring it back, until finally we told him that it was needed for something else in the village. When he brought it back, we could tell that he was quite upset. Asking him what the problem was, he responded: "You don't like me. You want that axe back, and I need it!" What a mistake we had made. For weeks he either ignored us or responded in a very cold fashion. Trying to explain to him that we were sorry made no difference. When our colleague, Claude, who was working among Trios, but in a village on a different river, visited us, we brought up this matter. He offered to go and talk to the man and find out why he had this attitude and why he thought that I did not like him. "Fred (Peledi was my name in Trio) does not like me, because he wanted his axe back, and I still had to cut my garden! If I cannot cut my garden, there will be no food for me and my wife, and my children!" he replied. Wow, what a mistake we had made.

Many years later, when the Trios had learned the word 'culture' and the concept of it, we admitted that we had to learn the Trio culture and how it differs from other cultures. Then we told them about the mistake that I had made in asking for that axe several times. They responded right away. It was something they knew about and had talked about for a long time. "No," they said, "that is not part of our culture. That is his culture and not ours. He does the same thing to us. Don't be sad about it!" Well, we were not sad anymore, because our relationship with that man was excellent. As a matter of fact, he had become my number-one language helper.

The same man also helped me along another line. Trying to learn more of the Trio language and culture and background, I asked him to tell me some stories of the Trios' former ways of life. That went well for a couple of hours, until he looked at me and said: "Brother! You came here to teach us God's Paper and the new life we have now. I don't want to talk about our former ways of life!"

Lesson quickly learned!

Going . . . ! A Sacrifice?

<u>Nationals providing things</u>

It probably is true in most, if not all, cultures, that people want to show their hospitality and appreciation by giving you something.

One of the first tokens of appreciation in the Aucaner tribe on the Cottica River came from the Captain of the village. On one of the first Saturdays in our house, Captain Walter came to us, to ask if anyone had brought us any meat that day. No, no one had done so. Then he went back to the village and some time later he came back with the hind quarter of a wild pig. The men had been hunting and brought back a number of these animals. There it was on the counter in our kitchen: bloody, with both hide and hair and toes. What an experience for both of us! Walter must have seen the look on Trudy's face. He quickly asked: "Shall I clean it for you?" Such a wonderful offer! Eventually Trudy became quite efficient in cutting up a whole deer or wild pig, and putting smaller portions in plastic bags, to put in our small freezer, in our kerosene refrigerator.

<u>Eating with Indians</u>

On our first river trip to go from the Trio village of Paloemeu to the Wayana village of Apetina we learned a lesson. We met a group of Wayana Indians at the bottom of one of the beautiful waterfalls. They invited us right away to have breakfast with them. It was probably eleven o'clock in the morning, and we had eaten breakfast already with our Trio companions, but we had learned already that it is very impolite to turn down an invitation to eat. So we ate with them as well. That kind of thing, adapting to a culture, spread rapidly within the tribe! We learned quickly!

When Trudy was busy in the clinic, from four in the afternoon until it started to get dark, I would walk through the village, to sit down with families and talk, and listen to their stories and sometimes personal problems. That was also a good time to learn more of their language and customs. But they would always ask me to eat with them. Even eating a few bites showed them that I was willing to be one of them and that I appreciated their hospitality.

Imagine visiting with maybe ten families on such a walk! Having a whole meal with each one would add to one's weight, but they were always satisfied when I took just a few bites and as a thank-you, said: "I am done!" or even a better response, "I am with stomach!"

We learned to do the same thing — to share our food. Normally, they could tell from a distance when we were eating as a family or having something to drink. They would usually stay away for a while. But if that was not the case, and they came into the house while we were eating, they would just sit in the Indian Room, and be very quiet. We started very quickly to share with them whatever we were eating.

We learned quickly!

<u>Pointing lips</u>

Trios were not used to pointing at something or someone with their fingers. I guess it is not polite in many cultures to point at another person either. But they all used to point with their lips. You know, those stuck-out lips, as if they wanted to kiss someone! But kissing they do not do!! Too bad!

It was something rapidly adopted by our whole family, as we talked to each other or to Indians. But we had to be very careful, once we were back in 'civilization', and had meetings in churches, on deputation. As if the Indian civilization is not a civilization! Imagine us doing that in churches, and I know we did it, without realizing it. Fortunately, nobody else noticed it, either. If they had, it might have taken us a lot longer to raise our support. Today we might still lose some support over it!

<u>Skin color</u>

It is amazing how quickly one can adjust to different kinds of people, ethnic groups and cultures. Sometimes, after having met a new person, we would talk about him or her. But then we began to notice that we could not even remember their skin color, or what ethnic group they were from. As a very small child, Rosyanne had become used to seeing only dark-colored people, and the only people she knew with light skins were us, her parents. Eva was one of the girls in the village, and she would regularly visit us and play with Rosyanne and carry her all over the mission station. After we had lived in Ricanau Moffo for a couple of weeks, we had a visit from a Dutch couple, who lived in the bauxite town of Moengo. Seeing them made our daughter cry, in a way we had not seen before. She was literally scared to death, seeing those white people.

One thing Rosyanne was not afraid of was being washed at our dock in the Cottica River. No problem to her, but it was quite an experience for Trudy. Was this the thing she would have to do every day? And was this where our daughter was going to grow up? Yes, it was, and she has many good memories!

"For the love of Christ constraineth us.." 2 Cor. 5:14

Chapter 18

This Is Not Work!

Trudy and I do not know how many times we have heard outsiders speak about the Indians in a very negative way. Tourists and other visitors from Paramaribo were convinced that Indians are lazy. It was either hear-say or some picture or article that had caused them to reach such a conclusion. Of course, there were those times when people were in the village, during the week, and saw some Indians, either in their hammocks, or all dressed up with long loin cloth and beads, sitting in some hut or walking through the village.

Such visitors were quick with their judgment. For example, there was a photographer who came and spent one day in the village. The man was gay, and wanted to prove that homosexuality exists everywhere, and is a natural thing. When he saw some Indian men in the village, holding hands, he had proof of his self-developed theory. Later on we received a copy of the magazine he worked for, and there was an article with all kinds of pictures, and his own conclusions. He did not realize that, in this culture and many others, it is quite acceptable for a man to hold hands with another man, and is not indicative of a homosexual relationship.

It is not true either that these Indians are lazy. Well, of course some are, as in every society. But who wants to call Indians lazy, when they build airstrips in the tropics, when the sky is blue and the temperature is way over 120 degrees? Together with them, we built three airstrips. As if that wasn't warm enough, they started burning the trees and branches and digging out the stumps, sometimes four feet deep, and rolling those big monsters off to the side into the fires. Our whole family joined in this effort. You should have seen Rosyanne and Artwin, around the age of three and four years, roll the smaller stumps and trunks of trees by themselves, while we were building the first airstrip at Tepoe!

As we did this for several weeks, drinking gallons of whatever liquid was available, the thermometer registered 140 degrees one time, while working together with the Indians to build our third airstrip at the Bible Camp! Who would call these people lazy? Is it laziness for fifty-four people to haul four big canoes with tons of food and supplies and fuel and planting material over the river for three or four days, and then to carry it all through the jungle for up to three hours? What about bringing these same canoes over the waterfalls or pulling them over the rocks for hundreds of yards?

Then we will never forget the statement, made by Muta and some of the other men, when they looked at the remaining nine hundred feet of airstrip, still to be cleared from tree stumps. There were literally hundreds of stumps: small, large and very large ones. But this man said: "There are only five stumps left! Those only are work!" Those stumps were four feet wide and three or four feet deep in the ground. And the roots were intertwined with the roots of other trees. Taking out those five stumps was the only work they still had to do! I guess most of us Westerners would have called a company to come and remove just one of the middle-size stumps.

How often has the Lord reminded us of the words: '...for the love of Christ constraineth us...'! The only reason the Indians wanted to build that Bible Camp and an airstrip in a virgin area of the jungle was to accommodate Indians from other tribes in Brazil, so they would be able to attend the annual one-month Bible School. The Trios did not consider it 'work' to travel four days up the river, and three or four days back, to pick up these people of other tribes so they could come to the Bible School. Before leaving the camp to pick them up, they had already built huts for them. What about those who came to the Bible Camp, to hear the teaching of 'God's Paper" and traveled up to three weeks to sit on hard benches, for four hours every morning? And sometimes that long again in the evening!

Thinking about Muta — we had known him first in the 1960's, when he was a young boy. Yes, he attended church with his parents and lived as all the other children of the tribe. We had witnessed his baptism. When the plan was made to build the Bible Camp on the Paloemeu river, he volunteered to help.

And he was an extremely hard worker! His role in organizing each Bible Camp was invaluable.

Years later, during one of those months of Bible Camp, a couple of elders came to talk to us. "We are going to talk to Muta!" they said. "About what?" we asked them. "We want to make him a deacon!"

That would be great, I thought. When I asked one of these men in the evening, if they had been able to talk to Muta, he said: "YES! We talked to him." "What was his answer?" was my next question.

"Muta said 'NO'. He would rather work than be deacon!" was their reply. Isn't that what a deacon is supposed to do? And Muta was and still is a hard worker. No wonder that they gave him the nickname: King Kong!

Peter said: "I go fishing!"....
They said: "We also go with thee!" John 21:3

Chapter 19

Hunting and Fishing

Duchesse, our Dalmatian, was a very special dog. She loved everybody, and was taller than all the other dogs in the village. Most of the dogs were being trained to hunt wild pigs. They were quite obedient to their owners, but could be very mean. As soon as we went outside, she followed us, but other dogs, who were not tied down on their platforms, showed up right away, showing their teeth and barking. Duchesse would just stand there and look at them. One by one the others would turn away and disappear.

But why would their teacher have a dog and not hunt with her? So the question came, one day, if the Indians could take Duchesse with them on one of their hunting days, which were Wednesdays and Saturdays. Off they went in one of our canoes, using our outboard motor.

It was about mid-afternoon when we heard the men come back from upriver. How embarrassed they were! Duchesse was not with them. The first shot, by one of them, scared her so much that she took off and did not come back even when they kept calling her. Fortunately, they did come home with plenty of meat.

Together we went upriver to look for Duchesse. The distance between the village and where they had gone into the jungle may have been about half an hour or so, by boat. But after about fifteen minutes, we saw our dog come swimming down the river. Putting her in the canoe, we could tell how happy she was to see us again. And our Indian friends were relieved!

On another occasion a large group of them took our canoe and put an old Mercury motor on it, which we had been given by our merchant-friend in Paramaribo, from whom we had purchased our first and second motors. Years before, this motor had been used by 'Operation Gwamba'. That was an effort to save animals in the area which flooded after a dam was put in the Suriname river. They left early in the morning, to make sure they could come home with lots of meat. The rains had started already and the river had swollen considerably. We had always made sure that outboard motors were securely fastened to canoes. However, that time, they had neglected to do that. After traveling upriver in that swift running water, they came to some whitewater. As the canoe went up and down a couple of times, "all of a sudden it was quiet," they said. The motor had been lifted off the transom and disappeared into the deep. No way to get it back. After that incident, each time they put an outboard motor on a canoe, several men would ask the 'motorman: "Did you tie it down well?" The motor stayed in the river for several months.

On subsequent trips, coming by where this had happened, everyone would show us the exact spot. Then one day, they decided to go back and look for it. The water had come down to the usual level. Rocks were visible again and the narrow passage in that part of the river did have enough water to get through. Tamenta was with us. In spite of his handicap — having one paralyzed leg — he was an excellent diver. It seemed as though he was able to get oxygen out of the water, like a fish. After several dives, he came back up and said: "I know where the motor is!"

With that information two other men dove in, with a long rope in their hands. It took a while, but when they came up again, they indicated that we could pull up the rope. Slowly the motor appeared above water and then was lifted into our canoe. What can you expect? This thing was old and had been well used before, and had been in the water for three months or more. However, after taking it back to the village, rinsing it out with more water, taking out the sand and leaves, cleaning the sparkplug and putting rich fuel in the tank, we pulled the starter cord only twice. It fired up right away! That motor got used for a long time!

There are times when the people did not have to go very far to get meat for the day or a couple of days. Deer would start roaming in their gardens. Even capybaras, a kind of water hog, a large rodent, would come into the camp. Capybaras can be very destructive. These animals also uprooted cassava roots and sweet potatoes. In the dark, these animals can be spotted with flashlights, and provide plenty of meat. They get eaten, instead of the banana trees being eaten by these animals.

A couple of weeks before Christmas, boatloads of Indians left to get lots of meat for the Christmas celebration. Christmas is celebrated for two days in that part of the country, as in many places in the world. Two large canoes came back from upriver two days before Christmas. We could see the big piles of smoked meat and fish from our porch. As soon as the women in the village saw the return of the canoes, they disappeared into the gardens, right across the airstrip, on the north side of the village. They needed to gather enough firewood to keep the smoked meat from spoiling, and flies from ruining it. Within five or ten minutes several of them came running back, and shouted, "There are pigs in the gardens!" Within moments most of the men ran across the airstrip, into the gardens. It did not take very long before we heard the first shot. Then more shots and more and more. It sounded like war. Then these men started appearing again, with wild pigs on their shoulders and around their necks. Now what?

All of the prey was cleaned on the rock in the river. Large pieces of the animals were put on the large tri-pots, which were quickly erected, to be smoked. Other pieces disappeared into regular pots and pans. There was more meat for the Christmas celebration than these more than three hundred people would be able to handle, although, when there is much to eat, they eat a lot! Then on December 26th, the mission plane came in and needed to pick up a patient less than one hour south of us. The plane was quickly filled up with about five hundred pounds of all kinds of smoked meat. It went to family members and others in a village situated on a creek. They did not have such an abundance of meat, and that village housed many more Trios and people of other tribes. Now Indians in both villages were praising God for His provisions. Joy among hundreds of people!

Many years later, when we were at the Bible School camp, something similar happened. The pastor of our "home church" that had helped to send us out as missionaries, Dan Skogen, was with us and was helping with the Bible teaching. He was teaching on the subject of the Tabernacle. At the end of his days of teaching, he even built a Tabernacle, actual size, with jungle material. It was still early in the morning. The second hour of teaching had just begun. While translating for Dan, who taught in English while I translated for him, I noticed that there was some unrest among the 150 students. When I asked what was going on, they pointed in the direction of the river on my left side and their right side. "Pigs!" they said. Then one of the leaders ordered them to be quiet, because we were teaching God's Paper. My response was: "If God sends you meat, don't let it go!"

The building was empty in five seconds. People ran toward their huts to get shotguns, bows and arrows, machetes and clubs. Those who could still get into one of the many canoes, did so. Others followed by just jumping into the river with whatever 'weapon' they had picked up. At that time the herd split into two groups. Some of the pigs swam back to the riverbank from where they had come, while others continued to swim downriver through the rapids, but a number of them just kept swimming around in the river. When all the activity was over, we had thirty-three wild pigs which needed to be cleaned, cut up, and made ready for cooking and smoking. Teaching was over for that day!

Trudy went down to the river to help the women with their work. Remember how she was afraid in 1964 to touch the hind quarter of a wild pig, when the captain of the village came to our house, to give us enough meat for one week or more?

Later that afternoon we had two large buckets with wonderful lean meat. The meat grinder did its work. No, I should say that differently. Trudy started cutting up the larger pieces of meat and mixing it with spices. I did the grinding and Dan made the patties. Just when it started to get dark, everybody assembled to thank the Lord and to eat those almost two hundred 'pig burgers'.

The meat of another wild pig we also enjoyed. One afternoon, on a walk through the village, I went across the airstrip to visit people who lived in that area. As I put my first steps on a small trail, leading to their huts, I saw Enkiman coming toward me with a domesticated wild pig on a rope, his pet. He had kept it and fed it for a long time, but now it had become difficult to handle, so close to other huts and people and children.

"What are you going to do with your pet and your dogs?" I asked him. "I cannot keep the pet pig any longer and I want to train my dogs to hunt wild pigs!" was his answer. I have no idea what got into our Duchesse. She approached that pig, grabbed it on its back, shook it several times and then let go. The pig was dead. How embarrassed I was! Our dog had never done anything like that. Never bitten anyone, never been mean to other dogs. "Brother, I am sad. My pet killed your pet!" I said.

He began to laugh and said: "That is what my dogs were going to do anyway! That is why I wanted to go to the end of the airstrip! "Do you want the meat?" he asked. They themselves would never eat the meat of an animal that they had kept for so long as a pet.

"They have not known, nor understood...." Isaiah 44:18

Chapter 20

Visitors in the Indian Villages

There were plenty of visitors. We were still living in Paloemeu, before we all moved to the new village of Përëru Tëpoe. Some tourists came to visit the Indians and see how they lived and what life in the jungle is like. Some were very polite and inquisitive, ready to learn.

Others had a critical attitude. After one of those tourist groups arrived on a Sunday, one man ran down the airstrip to the mission station. As soon as I met him, he started yelling and criticizing: "Why do you make these people enclose their huts with all that wood? That is not Indian-like!" I tried to explain to him that this is what Indians do. They cut long pieces of firewood, and enclose the sides of their huts, so when it rains and the wind blows, things in the hut don't get wet, like their hammocks and mosquito netting.

Then he criticized us for letting Indians wear mirrors. "That is not Indian-like, either!" he told me. No, I guess, many years ago they did not have mirrors. But once they had received them, they discovered that it was a nice way to decorate themselves, together with their beads and feathers.

"Why do you allow them to kill these birds, and use the feathers?"

"Well, sir, that is what Indians have done for many years, not only in Suriname, but in other countries in the world, too, including the United States!" was my explanation. After I had answered a few more of his ridiculous questions, his attitude began to change.

Many of these negative attitudes were created by some journalists who hated missionaries. They believed that missionaries ruin the Indian culture. If drunkenness and immorality and infanticide and other killing is part of their culture, yes, that has changed. That is what the Gospel, the Word of God, will do.

After all, these journalists had written stories stating that we missionaries were not there to help the Indians, but for the gold.

One newspaper in Paramaribo had been publishing articles about these things. And the proof was that the pilot would go home after a flight, on his Vespa scooter. On the backseat he usually had a small package, sometimes bigger, sometimes smaller. According to the newspaper articles, the packages contained the gold that missionaries were finding or taking from the Indians! The truth of the matter was that there was mail in those packages that we and other missionaries sent with the pilot, letters to be mailed from the city. Of course, we had no post office in the Indian villages.

On one occasion an Indian, from another river and a different tribe, came to show me a small jar with something in it. He wanted to know if I would give him money for the gold nuggets in that container. We had heard about gold fields in the part of the country where he was from, and that gold nuggets were spit out at times by the equipment that was used to mine gold. Indians followed the operation and found the nuggets. Certainly we did not want to get involved in this kind of criminality, as we believed it was. How the Lord protected us in this matter, as well! If we had not heard about this practice on the other side of the country, we would have believed what our 'outlandish' visitors were trying to explain to us.

When we think about these experiences, we do laugh. One of the ladies who came for a Sunday with the other tourists, came to our house and seemed to like it. She too wanted to buy some authentic Indian souvenirs, but when it was time to leave, she asked: "Are you going back to the city with us?" "No!" was our reply. "We stay here, because we live here!" "You mean you live here with these people and expose your children to this kind of culture? It is dangerous! How do you dare?" she said. "Madam, it is safer here, with these people, than it is for you in the city!" These missionaries are funny people, she must have thought.

Let us tell you about this writer for the National Geographic magazine. He had heard about the Akuriyo tribe that had been discovered in 1968, and that this tribe would be coming to the village of Tepoe. He wanted to write an article and photographers would come later to take the pictures for that magazine. However, he was misinformed, as there were no Akuriyos in the village yet. So he wanted to write something else, but about the village of Tepoe. "Could he speak to the chief?" we were asked. Sure, Tamenta is here and he would be very happy to come and meet this panakiri, white man. But as Tamenta sat down in our house, the man made his first statement to us, just so we knew who he was.

"Let me say, first of all, that I am an atheist!" he said.

"I do not believe in atheists!" was my reply. That took his breath visibly away. "You may deny the existence of my God, but you do not believe that everything around us just happened, do you?" I continued. "Well, you know what I mean. It started somehow by some power or whatever!" was his reply. "If that is the case, where did that power come from?" I asked him.

By that time he had become a little more antagonistic. "You mean to tell me that these people were unhappy people before you told them about the Bible and Jesus? And that they are happy now?" he said. I was ready to answer him, by telling how the Trios had changed: They were no longer practicing infanticide, and there was no longer the constant drunkenness, immorality, and fighting and killing. There was no longer the fear of being cursed by another tribe's people and witchdoctors. Now one could see evidence of loving care for one another, love for their children, and a desire for larger families.

But then, as if the Lord stepped in, to let me know that I should not be answering that question, I realized that I needed to let Tamenta answer him. So I asked this omniscient atheist if he would restate his question and maybe divide it in two parts, or so. He did!

One: "Were you unhappy people before?"
Two: "Are you happy people now, because of the Bible and God?"
I translated the questions. There was no response from Tamenta for maybe a minute or a little longer.

Then he said: "No, we were not unhappy people!" O my! What had I done? Were we being misunderstood? Then, after a pause, Tamenta said: "But with what we know now and have heard about God, we realize how unhappy we used to be!" Personally, I could not have answered it any better. Poor white sophisticated man. This answer floored him.

How could he say anything against this? His questions were answered in such a wise and wonderful way, by a member of what the outside world of 'sophisticated' people think are 'uncivilized and uninformed' jungle people.

'Going into all…the jungles…!"

Chapter 21

More Outreach

After reaching out to people of their own tribe in Brazil, and being involved in reaching that stone-age tribe, the Akuriyos, the Trio church followed up their missionary vision by visiting villages on the coast of Suriname. Some members went to French Guyana and others to Brazil.

In 1986, after we had spent a period of teaching in the village of Tepoe, interior fighting started. Soon the village was deserted, as the Trios fled up the river and congregated in the jungle. They built huts a short distance from the bank of the Upper Tapanahony River, at a place upriver from rapids and difficult passages.

In case they heard outboard motors traveling in their direction, they still would have had time to extinguish any fires, but they could not be noticed from the river. Some of the Trios had been hired by government troops and some others by a large rebelling group. Of course, Indians know their way around on the rivers and in the jungle, and were very useful to these fighting parties.

Members of these two groups were also present in the village of Tepoe, at times. On the airstrip that we had built with the Trios, there was some weaponry to shoot down any plane that was trying to land there.

When we returned to that village in 1992, after the fighting had stopped, we wondered in what condition we would find our house and all our belongings, which had been stored away in a large room, protected by chicken wire, from mice and rats. No, neither army people nor members of the other group had touched the place and no one had asked whose house it was. Did they even see that house, or did the Lord close their eyes to it? A few other people from the outside, who had been there for special projects, had lost everything they had left behind.

But as the hostilities got closer to the village, a few families decided that it was time for them to return to Brazil, back to the places from where they had come many years earlier, in the early 1960's.

Let me tell you, first of all, about one of these first families. Naki was the head of the family. We were told that he was a Pianagotto, from a different tribe not existing anymore. After he had come to the small Trio village on the Paloemeu river and heard the Gospel, preached by Morgan Jones, a pastor from New Jersey, he got all excited. This was something his relatives in Brazil needed to hear, too. Yes, he was excited, but not saved.

If only more saved people would be half as excited about the Gospel as Naki was, exciting things would happen in this world, and many people who have not yet heard the Good News of Jesus Christ, and His love for our world, could be reached. Naki was a man who had heard the good news, but was not yet born again; he made that long trip back to tell his family members and others in their villages in Brazil about what he had heard.

Doesn't that remind you of the Samaritan woman in John 4:29? "Come and see...!" Actually, after many years of my teaching, we heard Naki preach on that passage. Yes, we learned from those people, to whom we had the privilege of teaching the Word of God, as we translated portions of Scripture little by little, in the 1960's and 1970's.

After having read that passage, he started explaining it verse by verse. Then suddenly he asked a question: "How many people do you think this woman brought to the Lord!" We were astonished! How would he know? Then he proceeded to explain this woman's life style again: she was a sinner, who had had five husbands already and was now living with a sixth man. "Do you think that woman had a good name in that village? Do you think her words would have been respected by anyone in that village? Of course not! We look down on a woman like that. That is how we used to live!" he said.

Then he made this beautiful application: "But this woman had a chance to at least speak to these five husbands she had had, and the one man she was living with now!" "So all of us do have people we can talk to because we have some kind of a relationship with them! And look what happened: They left the village and came to HIM, to Jesus!"

Yes, lots of these men were used by God in many ways. These Indians were taught, and they began to teach, and the Word of God spread all over that region.

After translating the book of Jonah for them, we mimeographed it. (Do you know what a mimeograph machine is?) Then we took the time to go through it every morning for an hour or more. Several weeks later, when everybody was back from taking 'a vacation' in a hunting camp, we were in the Sunday morning service.

Naki had been assigned to teach the Bible lesson and he knew it because his name was on a weekly schedule, put together by one of the other church leaders, and mimeographed by us. After the initial singing, reciting of Bible verses and prayer, one of them read the first chapter of that small book of Jonah. Now it was Naki's turn to speak. "Have you heard the story of Jonah? It was just read to you. And if you cannot read it, at least you have heard it now, after our teacher taught us a long time ago. What was Jonah's three-fold sin?" he said. Wow! I had never taught them to come up with a three-part outline when preaching or teaching. I had learned the concept in Bible School in France. How had he come up with that idea?

He continued: "That is what some of you would do! You see Jonah was told by God: to go, but Jonah refused. Actually, while he should have gone in the direction where the sun comes up, he went in the direction where the sun goes down. That was his first sin.

His second sin was that he did not use what God had given him, his money, in a way that honored God. Instead, he used that money to flee from the presence of God. Now some of us have money, too. And instead of using it for the Lord, we buy pots and pans, and loin cloth and beads and many more things. Often things we do not really need! That is why there is not much money in 'God's Box' [the money container in the church]. Jonah's third sin was that he did not pray. He was God's servant who, instead of praying, was asleep. And those who had not trusted God were trusting their own gods, and were praying to them. They had to wake Jonah up and make him ashamed!"

This is the message many Christians need to hear! And put into practice!

PRAYING, GIVING, GOING

As you are reading these things, can you understand why Trudy and I never considered missionary work a sacrifice?

Then we think back to the days when my dad jokingly said to Trudy and me, "And when you go to that jungle, you will be sitting on orange crates!" We will never forget that statement. Our answer was: "So what?" To be honest, we never sat on orange crates. We did sit on other things, and we used orange crates for some time as book cases and to put our dishes in. "So what?" In those days my dad was an elder in the local church in the Netherlands. He knew much about the Bible, but was not yet born again. He had a job that paid well, and he wanted to see all of his four sons and three daughters able to live a life like he and mom did, and we children did at home. As a matter of fact, my dad wanted to see me go into the business world. Well, the Lord's work is the best 'business' to be involved in!! We have the best Employer in the world. HE pays better too: ETERNAL DIVIDEND!

And now I am married to my EMPLOYER'S DAUGHTER! When we got married, the pastor spoke on the verse in Romans 8: 31, "If God be for us, who can be against us?" And he pointed out that God is for all of us, and wants all of us to know Him! God has been for us in all these years of missionary service!! And He has provided all our needs and many of our wishes for more than fifty years.

SACRIFICE or INVESTMENT

Is investing a sacrifice? NO! There is interest coming!
People invest, because of what the result will be.

So it is with missions:
- you forego certain things.
- you gain something, and
- you lay up treasures in heaven!

It is easy to sing: Wherever HE leads, I'll go! But do you really mean that?

"CHOOSE ye this day...!"

CHAPTER 22

Going! A Sacrifice?

That is the title of this book.

That is the question we want to ask you, dear reader!

That is the question we have for those who have decided already what they want to do with their lives.

That is the question we want to ask those who have not decided yet what they want to do with their lives.

Quite a question to ask, isn't it? It was the important challenge Joshua gave to the Israelites, after he had lived a life of serving His Lord: "Choose ye this day whom you will serve." There are questions we must ask ourselves, if we are serious about our walk with the Lord, because some of those questions may be asked by others, or perhaps by the Lord Himself.

We have been sharing with you how the Trios and other tribes have responded to the Word of God.

One of the first parts of the Bible I had the privilege of translating for the Trios was the book of Jonah. I did the translation together with Pisere, who was the leader of the Tepoe Church for many years. He was the son of a chief of that tribe, in that region of the jungle, the south of Suriname and parts of Brazil. His father had been murdered by two other men from his tribe, who eventually came to know the Lord.

The book of Jonah tells us about God's will for Jonah, and the mission God had sent him on. While we were working on those chapters, Pisere suddenly stopped me and asked a question: "Brother! What were you doing before Morgan (they called him Muksi) came to us?" My answer was a true and simple one: "I was studying God's Papers, to become a 'sent one', a missionary!" And as we continued that conversation, it became clear to me why he had asked that question. Jonah had refused to answer the call from God.

Pisere wanted to know whether, perhaps, there had been a person like Jonah, in the days of his father — a person whom God had wanted to send to the Trios, way before, but who had 'fled from the presence of the Lord'! Why did Pisere hear the Good News about God's love, and the coming of Jesus Christ, while his father never heard? His father had lived the same way as he had: fishing in the same rivers, hunting on the same trails, planting cassava and banana trees, and many things like that. But nobody had come during his father's lifetime!

In those years in the 1960's, the Trios were concerned about a tribe in Brazil. "They are mean people and they are killers!" they told us. The opportunity never presented itself, at that time, for the Trios to make that long trip, which might have taken weeks or, possibly, months.

When we had the opportunity, many years ago, to go to the main village of the Apalai people, Trudy and I walked through that village. Approaching a hut, right beside the trail, we saw an Indian with his wife and two children. We did not know who he was. But he introduced himself and his family to us. "I am...!" and he gave us his name, and the name of the tribe he was from. That was the tribe we had heard about, more than forty years before. Then he proceeded to say to me: "I know you! I met you in the village of Alalaparu! You remember the people who had come, to that village, to revenge the death of someone murdered in Brazil?"

Sure, I remembered. Missionary Claude was on an expedition, looking for the Akuriyo Indians. His wife Barbara was alone in the village. We received the request from her by radio, to come and assist the people in that village in protecting a certain person. He had been involved, many years before, in the killing of a man from a different tribe. The same plane that took me to Apalaparu brought that particular Indian to Tepoe, where Trudy was with our children.

Every night we were up. Indians with flashlights and walkie-talkies were everywhere in the village and on some hills around the village. We were in constant communication with each other. Thankfully, nothing happened. We never found out what happened to these 'unwelcome visitors'!

That event was remembered by this man. He was from the tribe that wanted to revenge the killing of a member of his tribe.

Now you need to understand the background of this 'revenge killing'. In the Bible we are told to love our enemies. However, in this particular tribe, and other tribes as well, you show your love for your loved one by killing a relative of the murderer. If you do not revenge that murdered loved one, you demonstrate that you do not love your relatives.

The father of the children we met that day in Brazil, had lost his father, as he was killed in this process of 'revenge killing'. He shared with us that he was not willing to continue this string of killings. He had fled to Alalaparu. And it was there, in that village, that he came to know the Lord. Since that time he had returned to Brazil.

"Where is your tribe?" we asked him.

"We finished ourselves!" was his answer.

"What do you mean by that?" I asked him.

"This killing continued for a long time! I did not want to be part of it, although I should have revenged my father's death," he said.

Our next question was: "How many are left? We have met you now; we also met a woman from your tribe in the Bible School in Suriname!" He could not tell us the number of people left from his tribe at that time, but a couple of days later, during that Bible Conference in Brazil, he gave us a piece of paper with thirty-nine names on it. A tribe of probably hundreds of people had almost been wiped off the face of the earth — people who had not heard the Good News about Jesus, and went into Eternity without Him. Fortunately, there were a few who were reached with the Gospel!

Earlier on in this book, we shared about how our support came in to enable us to work among the Indians. All we could do was pray. There was no email in those days, no letters could be sent out, and there were no deputation meetings.

Nevertheless, God provided a group of people who decided to support us. Among that number, let us share with you a few words about two supporters who stand out to us in a particular way.

There was Nick, as we called him, who together with his family had come to Suriname in 1964, to work for Alcoa, the American Aluminum Company. Nick was a licensed preacher in the USA. His deepest thoughts, about why he did not go into the ministry but preferred to have a good job and make lots of money, probably only Nick knew. But while in Suriname and after meeting missionaries working with these Indian tribes, he and his wife, Alice, decided to go back to the States for further Bible training. Then they came back to Suriname, to serve as missionaries, ministering to missionaries and Guyanese immigrants. You see? Nick was a bit like Jonah, to begin with. The big difference is that Nick, and his wife, rejoiced in obeying the Lord for the rest of their lives.

Nick had a colleague, Jack, working for the same company in Suriname. He started supporting us at the same time as Nick and Alice did. Once we were back in the city of Paramaribo, we spent a whole day with him, and he showed us the power plant that was being built. While standing on that dam in the Suriname River, Jack began to open up to us about his life and his career and the good job he had, although he was close to retirement at that time. "I knew, when I was younger, that the Lord wanted me in His service. I did not answer that call, but I made a lot of money! I pray for you missionaries, and I can support you!" he said. Then the tears started flowing from his eyes. He had missed God's goal and purpose for his life. Such words and tears are hard to take. He had reached 'the point of no return!'

Wasn't he talking about what Pisere was asking?

What were you doing when the Lord was calling you?
Or could the Lord be calling you now?

Edwards Brothers Malloy
Ann Arbor MI. USA
August 23, 2017